'Samantha Lane is an expert in her f
to. If you want to know everything th
ing with young people, this is the book to get.'

> — **Michael Grandage CBE**, *Artistic Director*
> *of the Michael Grandage Company, UK*

This is a very useful guide for practitioners and teachers with
some really clear advice about how to direct plays with young
people, written in an accessible style by a highly respected
practitioner from one of London's leading theatres.'

> — **Professor Helen Nicholson**, *Royal Holloway,*
> *University of London, UK*

This is an immensely useful guide to the nuts and bolts of exactly
what a director does and how to apply the best professional prac-
tices working with young people.'

> **Rupert Goold**, *Artistic Director of*
> *the Almeida Theatre, UK*

play with a young cast is both a challenging and
experience. *Directing Young People in Theatre* guides you
the entire process, from choosing or devising a play, to
rehearsing and staging it and reflecting on the whole
from professional directors and exercise sug-
ughout will help both you and your cast to
y and take full advantage of rehearsals and
and accessible, this book is the ideal com-
wishing to stage a play with young people –
youth workers, to Applied Theatre students
directors.

ve interviews with:

Michael Attenborough • Matthew Dunster
obert Icke • Indu Rubasingham • Lyndsey Turner

e is Director of Projects at the Almeida Theatre,
tion Associate for the Michael Grandage Company,
UK. She is also a drama practitioner and Course Director for the
Almeida                                                    in Applied
Theatre                  **KA 0393442 X**                 l of Speech
and Dram

# Directing Young People in Theatre

## A Guide to Staging Plays with Young Casts

Samantha Lane

 palgrave

First published 2015 by
PALGRAVE

Palgrave in the UK is an imprint of Macmillan Publishers Limited, registered in England, company number 785998, of 4 Crinan Street, London, N1 9XW.

Palgrave Macmillan in the US is a division of St Martin's Press LLC, 175 Fifth Avenue, New York, NY 10010.

Palgrave is a global imprint of the above companies and is represented throughout the world.

Palgrave® and Macmillan® are registered trademarks in the United States, the United Kingdom, Europe and other countries.

ISBN 978–1–137–34048–1    hardback
ISBN 978–1–137–34047–4    paperback

This book is printed on paper suitable for recycling and made from fully managed and sustained forest sources. Logging, pulping and manufacturing processes are expected to conform to the environmental regulations of the country of origin.

A catalogue record for this book is available from the British Library.

A catalog record for this book is available from the Library of Congress.

Typeset by MPS Limited, Chennai, India.

Printed in China

*To my amazing husband, James,*
*and my beautiful girls, Charlotte and Isabelle*

# Contents

# Foreword

A fact politicians rarely appreciate is the way in which we shape and influence the lives and personalities of young people today, will define what kind of society we shall have in the future. The connection between education and the creative arts is clearly not valued by the present government, given their recent shameful omission from the national curriculum. This merely reflects their attitude to the arts in general, via the shrinkage of university arts and humanities departments, the closure of libraries and the massive cutbacks in funding to arts institutions the length and breadth of the country.

When I arrived at the Almeida Theatre in 2002, there was no formal link to the world of education. So I set up a department and established a number of principles upon which it was to be founded. Firstly, our understanding of education would lie in the Latin word itself "educo" – I lead out. Its primary purpose is to provide an arena in which young people could express themselves. I was not interested in the conventional definition and application of "education" – namely cramming young people full of facts and arming them with exam techniques. Hence my reason for naming our department Almeida Projects, with the emphasis on the practicality, on the excitement of the new approach, and on constantly starting again and stepping out into the unknown. Secondly, I wanted Almeida Projects to be umbilically linked to what we produced on our main stage. Not, I hasten to add, as a giant marketing exercise but as a way of convincing young people that what we did on that stage was genuinely relevant to their lives and experiences. Thirdly, I wanted no distinction in quality between the professionals we employed in our theatre and those we hired to work with our young people. I wanted no sense that they were in a marginal B division; all the directors, writers, designers and actors were to be people I would readily employ on our main stage.

Not only was the work in our local secondary schools massively valued by teachers (endorsed by them all choosing to pay for the work when finally we had no option but to charge a contribution towards it), but the Almeida now has over 500 members of its Young Friends of the Almeida Scheme, composed of school leavers who actively want to continue their creative work with the theatre into adulthood. I have witnessed, at first hand, young people become quite literally different people; people with a new identity, no longer self-obsessed but collectively and socially aware, no longer cynical but positive and optimistic, no longer destructive but creative; their communication skills hugely enhanced, and their self-confidence and self-esteem utterly transformed.

But this does not happen by magic; it needs vision and leadership. From the moment I met Sam Lane, I knew we needed what she had; energy, passion, articulacy, charm and an instinctive intelligence. Perhaps most important for all, her joy in the work was evidently rooted in a realistic, down-to-earth unsentimental practicality.

Her book reflects her determination to locate and stimulate the creativity of young people; her commitment to provide them with the very best artists with whom to collaborate; her absolute respect for the rights of young people to determine the circumstances and nature of their own work, coupled with an equally unapologetic commitment to confront laziness, sloppiness or lack of self-discipline, wherever it might appear.

It is entirely typical of her espousal of high standards and her refusal to allow young people's work to be worthy, amateurish or second best, that her book is shot through with insights and observations from top theatre professionals. As far as she is concerned, we are all involved in the practical act of creating theatre to the highest possible standards. Collectively cohesive, artistically ambitious, produced with a generosity of spirit, I know of no finer testimony or tribute to her work than the extraordinary achievements of the young people she inspires. Her book now provides a unique and invaluable insight into her methodology, expertise and vision.

In a world where we hear of little else but deficits, money and materialism, this book dedicates itself unashamedly to the other half of our National Health; that which we don't see, can't touch and yet experience every day of our lives – our emotional, psychological, spiritual inner selves. In a word, our humanity.

If we are not to produce future generations of young people blunted, stunted and lethally desensitised, we need to stop polluting them as badly as we are our planet. Unlike politicians, we need to recognise, as Sam does, that inside every young person lies a core of creativity just waiting to be discovered, stimulated and expressed. What is at stake here is not something nebulous, airy fairy or esoteric, it's the future health of our society.

I commend this book to all those who love young people and possibly, you never know, to a future Secretary of State for Education.

*Michael Attenborough*

# Acknowledgements

I have worked as a facilitator and director of work by young people for many years, and during this time I have met numerous fantastic facilitators, teachers and directors. It is no secret that if you see an exercise you like, you steal it – sometimes outright, and sometimes adding your own twist. And so to those many fantastic facilitators, teachers and directors who I have had the privilege to work with – and whose exercises I have stolen – I thank you wholeheartedly for enriching and improving my practice.

I would like to thank the directors who I interviewed for the book, all of whom gave their time so generously. They were all incredibly open to sharing their practice and answering my questions freely and honestly. Without them, this book would not have been possible.

I also thank Pauline Tambling for her unwavering support and advice – truly the best mentor anyone could ask for.

And finally, I would like to thank my mum, dad and sister for always being there and supporting me in every endeavour; and my husband James for his endless enthusiasm and encouragement.

# 1
# Introduction

I first decided to write this book during a seminar with a group of trainee workshop leaders who were studying for the Post Graduate Certificate in Applied Theatre: Facilitation that the Almeida runs jointly with Royal Central School of Speech and Drama. Two students were talking about directing young people in plays, and asked me if I knew of any books that would help teach them how to do this. I racked my brains, but could only come up with a list of texts dedicated to directing theatre: *A Director's Craft* by Katie Mitchell; *A Director Prepares* by Anne Bogart; *Different Every Night* by Mike Alfreds; *So You Want to be a Theatre Director?* by Stephen Unwin; *The Theatre Director and the Stage* by Edward Braun and *Contemporary European Theatre Directors* by Dan Rebellato and Maria Delgado – to name a few, but none that dealt with taking a play from page to stage with a young cast. Of course, the savvy director might read any one of these and adapt the process to working with young people – and I wholeheartedly encourage this because this is exactly what this book aims to do: it focuses on the methodology of a select number of highly regarded professional theatre directors and examines how their practice can be mirrored and/or adapted to meet the challenges, and rewards, of working with young people rather than professionals.

Indeed, this book aims to provide a practical guide to help support those interested in directing theatre with young people. It will take you through the process of taking a play from page to stage, providing a basic framework for directing by drawing on the expertise of professional theatre directors, and simultaneously providing a range of exercises and tools to work with young people specifically. It is useful to anybody who wants to put on a play with a group of young people, from teachers of English or drama to Applied Theatre students; from youth workers who are interested in theatre to youth theatre directors; and even for professional directors who want to swap a professional cast for a young, un-trained one.

I have dedicated my entire career to creating work by, with and for young people, and to teaching others about the many different ways of doing this. But what do I mean by young people? For the purposes of the book, I will define young people as those of secondary school age (in the UK this is age 11 to 16 or 18, or year 7 to 11 or 13; in the US this is Junior High, grade 6 to 8, and High School, grade 9 to 12) – acknowledging the fact that after a certain age, although legally defined as a child, most children prefer the title of young person. However, all of the exercises in the book would be equally valuable for those who are a little younger and for those who are older (most of my work takes place with people aged 14 to 25), although they may well need adapting slightly, particularly for the very young.

It is also important here to define what I mean by theatre. Theatre is obviously a broad concept that encompasses an enormous body of work, and whilst I acknowledge this, and in no way want to narrow anyone's interpretation of theatre, for the purposes of this book I am interested in dramatic texts that are predominantly but not exclusively naturalistic. I want to help the reader lift that text from the page, providing a basic, step-by-step guide to the process, as well as a toolkit of rehearsal room exercises appropriate for young people to help ease this process. Even with the chapter on devising (Chapter 9), the focus is on using text as a starting point for this, and the final product also results in a play text. Again, the notion of devised work is also a broad concept, and there are many methods of approaching it, but this chapter focuses on how you can start with one form – a story or a novel – and finish with an entirely new one – a script.

I interviewed seven theatre directors for the book; six of whom I have had the privilege to work with at the Almeida Theatre, and one who is known to me through an actor friend. Throughout the book, the directors are intermittently referred to by either their full names or their first names. They are all predominantly directors of text-based theatre. They start with a play on the page, whether a classic text or new writing, and their job is to take it from page to stage. Two of the directors, however, I have interviewed specifically because they have also directed work that, although resulting in text, is devised and adapted from prose. One of the seven is currently an Artistic Director (Indhu Rubasingham); two have been Artistic Directors but are both now freelance directors (Michael Attenborough and Richard Eyre); one who is Associate Director at the Almeida (Robert Icke); one who is co-founder of renowned theatre company Complicite (Annabel Arden); and two who work as both associates and freelancers (Lyndsey Turner and Matthew Dunster). All of them have a huge array of experience directing a vast range of plays, yet they all work in the theatre in different ways. And each of them has their own unique approach to directing. Indeed, there is no science to this art form; no prescribed set of rules: just one person help- ing a group of other people to put on a play for an audience. As I have already mentioned, there are numerous books on the craft of directing, and there are numerous higher education providers who run courses on it, but, in my opinion, the best way to really work out how it is done is to get stuck in and do it. It is worth men- tioning here the distinction between an Artistic Director and a director. The former is somebody who runs a company or a build- ing, and he or she has to do so much more than just direct plays; indeed just because a director is good at directing a play, it does not mean that they will make a good Artistic Director. They pro- gramme what plays to put on, manage staff, report to the board and are often accountable for finances and business planning.

So what exactly is a theatre director, and what do they do? For most people, this conjures up the image of someone, very thespian in nature, standing in front of a group of actors, flouncing around and telling them where to stand and how to say their lines. Lyndsey Turner describes this type of director as a "point and shoot" direc- tor (Turner, 2012). Whilst there are some that do work this way, it is extremely rare in the professional world. The concept of the theatre director is a relatively new one and it did not come into its own until the twentieth century. Granted, as far back as Greek Theatre, Aeschylus oversaw the presentation of his tragedies; and there were the actor managers of Shakespeare's day; but these were the playwrights in the case of Aeschylus, and the leading actors in the Elizabethan era, who managed the company or the theatre's business and financial arrangements, and performed plays of their own choice in which they were usually the star. Both, although assuming a degree of overall responsibility, are a far cry from the role of director that we know today. However, as Lyndsey says:

> It is worth remembering that we did perfectly well without directors until about 100 years ago. Actor managers would programme plays, acting companies would rehearse them amongst themselves, and writers might take on some of the roles that a modern director inhabits. (Turner, 2012)

So why do we need them and what is their role? Indhu sees the role of the director as one of guidance:

> To lead with a vision, to be a collaborator, and to allow the best to come out of people in order to create an environment so that the vision is bigger than any one person. I think the role of the director is to guide and to steer the ship that will take everyone on this journey. (Rubasingham, 2012)

She believes that the director's role is not to dictate the choice but to limit the number of choices an actor can make at any given moment: "Instead of saying there is only one way of doing it, you are narrowing it down to a handful of ways of doing it" (Rubasingham, 2012). She also believes that it is important that the director can straddle both the world of the rehearsal room and the audience perspective. Lyndsey would concur. She sees the director as the person who shapes the intent of the production and tries to be the mediator between the audience and the performers, "and bat for both sides simultaneously" (Turner, 2012). For her the role is complex and multilayered:

> I am not entirely sure if I am being paid for my left brain, my right brain, or a particular combination of the two. But I think there is an expectation that the director is the person most likely throughout the rehearsal process to have a sense of where magnetic north is and how many degrees off we are at any given time. (Turner, 2012)

Mike sees the role of the director as a facilitator:

> It is not true that plays can speak for themselves. You are like a conductor; you are orchestrating. The actor has the score in front of him or her and you are trying to conjure the sound out. You have got to get their own interpretation and creative juices going. (Attenborough, 2012)

Richard agrees with the orchestral analogy, although the director is never seen by the audience in the same way that a conductor is, so the role is invisible. Matthew cites Rufus Norris, a fellow director, when he talks about the role of the director:

> Rufus said (and he means this in the positive and the negative), "the best thing about being a director, is everything is your fault." He means you are responsible for everything. Being the hub of responsibility is the role of the director. Everything comes to me and through me. (Dunster, 2012)

Annabel Arden believes "First and foremost the director must inspire and give confidence and be a guide to all the people involved, not just the actors but absolutely everybody," and she also believes that the director and the work are pretty much one and the same thing: "You have to embody the work. When people get angry and difficult and they direct it at you, it is not personal, they are just struggling with the work itself" (Arden, 2014). All of the professional directors see themselves as enablers. What is clearly crucial for them all is the relationships that they build with their actors and creative teams. That thespian director, standing in front of a group of actors, flouncing around and telling them where to stand and how to say their lines does not yield results. You need to gain the actors' trust, work with them, and be at once their confidante, friend, boss, social worker and teacher. You have to be different things to different people, and so flexibly, tact, thick skin and a good sense of humour go a long way – and that is all before any skill for taking words from a page and turning them into a play are even considered. However, if you get all of these things right, your actors will help to make this happen easily.

But remember, every single director is idiosyncratic and has their own process. As Richard says, "it is singular and it is appropriate to them, and I think it is disastrous to try and borrow somebody else's approach. You can be influenced by people but in the end it is you; it is your thoughts, your feelings, your imagination, and your personality that is going to be exhibited as part of the piece of work" (Eyre, 2013). Lyndsey agrees:

> To some extent, I am probably the sum of the people I have assisted: I owe a huge debt to Dominic Cooke, Ian Rickson, Katie Mitchell, James Macdonald and Jeremy Herrin in terms of evolving a process which works for me. But ultimately you can only direct from your own point of view, and if you are helping an actor to shape the behaviour of a character, it is inevitable that the way you see the world will bring itself to bear on that discussion. (Turner, 2012)

One thing that was patently obvious when interviewing the directors, was how passionate they were about their jobs. Indhu likes the fact that theatre tells stories, and believes in its transformative power. For Richard, directing enables him to create a surrogate family where he gets to choose the members of the family and he gets to be head of that family. Lyndsey sees it as a real privilege; "to invite a group of people to sit in the dark watching another group of people inhabiting characters who have previously only existed on a page, and to somehow pull that transaction off is a fantastic honour" (Turner, 2102). Matthew knows that he likes being a director better than being a playwright or being an actor or even being a teacher, and he enjoys the challenge, although he admits to finding the level of responsibility exhausting. Robert describes it as, "inexhaustibly fulfilling" (Icke, 2014), and Annabel says that she "cannot remember ever wanting to do anything except work in the theatre" (Arden, 2014).

But what about the role of the director of young people? And how does knowing the thoughts and opinions of the professional directors help? Like the professional director, the director of young people must find his or her own process, and knowing how others do it will only help to inform the choices that they make. And whilst the director of young people can borrow some of the techniques of a professional director, he or she has the added challenge of doing the same job but with an untrained, often large, cast – and so may need to adapt these techniques to make them appropriate. Indeed, the experiences and tips of the professional directors in the book should be considered as a benchmark – a number of possible ways of doing it that you may well adopt, but also as a departure point, giving you the freedom to say, "I'm going to do it a different way."

It would be natural for the untrained or inexperienced director to assume that a professional theatre director has the skills and experience to direct any group of actors, no matter how experienced, but the reality is often far from the truth. Most professional directors, whilst at home with professional actors or drama students, are not equipped with the necessary skills and techniques to work with a group of young people. I remember Bob Carlton, Artistic Director at the Queen's Theatre, from 1997 to 2014, once telling me that he needed a megaphone to direct a community play, and that it was the most exhausting rehearsal period of his life – even though the company only met twice a week for a few hours! Needless to say, he handed the direction of the community plays over to me, the Education Manager at the time. Equally, one might assume that drama teachers have the appropriate qualifications to direct a group of young people. Whilst they have the training and experience of working with young people, and all of the challenges that this entails, very few have had formal training in the art of directing. I was first alerted to this fact when a teacher friend of mine was mystified by the practical examination results of her students – she thought they had done well but the examiner marked them poorly. She went on to tell me that she was expected to direct her Advanced Level (a general certificate of education, studied over two-years in years 12 and 13 in the UK) students in a full scale production, despite the fact that her teacher training did not cover directing in any way. In fact, most drama teachers – a majority of whom are expected to direct the school plays as well as plays for the curriculum – have either just picked up directing skills on an ad hoc basis, or have adopted the most logical way that they can to putting on a play, finding their own approach as they go along. And many of them can be defined as "point and shoot" directors – not necessarily flouncing thespians, but certainly those who tell their actors where to stand and how to say their lines. As Richard Eyre said,

> When you start as a director, it is like puppets at the toy theatre – you want little figures so that you can move them around the stage and there will not be a traffic jam (Eyre, 2013).

But this approach can be counterproductive. When working with professionals, the director has a blank canvas and a willing, and carefully selected, cast of trained actors at his or her disposal. When directing young people, the director can be faced with multiple unknowns. He or she may know the actors, maybe having taught them before and even handpicking those that they perceive to be the most skilled in performance; or they might have a group who chose to study drama but are not yet confident performers, or worse still, those who chose the subject because they thought it would be easy but are completely uninterested. And remember, even seemingly skilled performers can be a challenge as their talent can be raw and unharnessed and certainly not trained, and, whilst exciting, poses a whole new set of challenges. Furthermore, young people are unpredictable. There may be behavioural issues, attendance and punctuality issues, pushy parents, a range of ages and ability, poor group dynamics, lack of experience – in performing and life – to name a few. Yet despite these additional challenges, anyone new to directing can learn a great deal from those with extensive experience of doing it.

It has become one of my key ambitions, as an artist who has dedicated my entire career to working with young people in theatre, to highlight this often unseen and forgotten work. There are a growing number of professionals now working in this field, and I hope that collectively we can raise the standard and status of working with young people in the industry, as well as introduce new people to it. I want to end the days where working with young people is viewed as secondary, or as a stepping stone, to the real work, and for people to realise that it is rewarding and artistically challenging in its own right. If this book can go some way towards helping others to realise the power and potential of high quality theatre making with young people, then I will be a step closer to reaching that ambition. And I hope that you find both the experience of the professionals and the practical exercises and pointers in the book useful on your journey of taking a play from page to stage.

# 2
# Choosing a Play

This chapter focuses on the daunting task of choosing a play to put on. Whilst it cannot make the decision for you, it gives useful insight into how professional directors make their choices and offers suggestions for how you might source a play text. There is also a set of questions to consider before making your choice, designed to make the job a little easier.

## Commissioning new plays and/or devising

When directing theatre with young people, one of the most difficult choices I have to make is which play to put on. The groups that I work with can range in size between 5 and 80 participants, and there is a serious shortage of existing and appropriate good plays for casts of a big size. I tend to overcome this problem by commissioning a playwright to write a brand new play for the young people to perform, or, if there is not a budget for this, by devising work with them – this way, the cast will have a sense of ownership of the piece and there will not be any issues with the play not having enough parts. Sometimes these are straightforward commissions, at other times they are more process driven, for example Almeida LAB. This is a project where young people, through a series of exploratory workshops, examine the resonances that existing plays (in this model specifically the current season of Almeida plays) have on their own lives in order to generate material for the writer. The end result is a play for these young people to perform – one that has been informed and

9

shaped by them. This has provided a bank of plays for young people, with casts ranging from 15 to 25, by high profile writers like Tanya Ronder, Robin French, John Donelly, Rebecca Prichard and Ros Wylie. However this model is a very specific one that requires financial backing and a degree of risk in relation to the quality and appropriateness of the final product. The play is not written when you start the journey, which can be a terrifying prospect. However, this could equally be the excitement and challenge that you are looking for.

Lyndsey Turner mostly works in new writing so the plays that she wants to direct have not yet been written. She says:

> I want to make theatre that speaks about how we live and how the institutions and ideas that govern our society shape our behaviours and relationships. I think that this is best done with new work. I tend to work with writers from a fairly early stage of the writing process, through successive drafts of a script into production, so I have a long standing relationship with that script and that writer. I am interested in plays that feel urgent or necessary in terms of contributing to a conversation about how we live and why we do what we do. (Turner, 2012)

The wonderful thing about working with a writer, specifically through a model like LAB, is that the stimuli for exploration can be anything and everything, giving the director scope to examine themes and ideas that he or she is interested in.

If you opt to devise, a good starting point is an existing story (for more details on this process, see Chapter 9 on Devising, where both Robert Icke and Annbel Arden start with novels that are adapted into plays).

## Having no, or limited choice

For some directors of young people, there may not be scope for choice of play. It may be dictated by the organisation that hires you or, for teachers, it may be a curriculum requirement. This can also be true for professional directors. Indeed, it is a common misconception that choosing a play to direct is a matter of personal taste. Many professional directors are hired by artistic directors to direct a play not of their choosing. And even when an established director is given the opportunity to select their own play, or is fortunate enough to run their own theatre, the choice is still not entirely down to personal taste. Does the play fit the theatre's programme, for example? Does it complement the season of work? Does it suit the size of the venue and the style of the space? Can the theatre afford it? Is it a risky choice like a new piece of writing by an unknown playwright? Or is it an all-singing, all-dancing extravaganza and guaranteed box office hit?

Leading a building means that an Artistic Director has to think less about what he or she personally finds interesting, and more about what the theatre needs and what the theatre's audiences need. Indhu Rubasingham is Artistic Director of the Tricycle Theatre, a theatre in the heart of Kilburn in North London that is well known for presenting plays that reflect the cultural diversity of its community. In programming her first season at the theatre, Indhu chose four plays that she felt really passionate about and she put them together to give a varied season that aimed to speak to different parts of that community:

> For example, I am doing *Arabian Nights*, which is the first family show that the Tricycle has done, because I want young people to come to the theatre. (Rubasingham, 2012)

For Indhu, or more specifically for the Tricycle, as well as being about her own personal taste, she also wants to present theatre that "holds up different lenses to the world and is always trying to show a different aspect to society" (Rubasingham, 2012). She believes theatre has a social responsibility to speak to a wide and varied demographic, and her programming reflects this.

## Freedom of choice and finding a connection with the play

In contrast to Indhu, Michael Attenborough, Artistic Director of the Almeida Theatre from 2002–13, had a less prescriptive ethos and consequently more freedom to choose a play of his own liking. Under Michael's tenure, the Almeida produced a diverse range of plays – both British and international drama – but there was no specific agenda. For Michael, it was a case of presenting the best theatre with some of the world's best artists. He acknowledges that there were plays that he thought the Almeida should put on and plays that he wanted to direct personally – and that they were not necessarily the same plays, but, with no political remit or strict definition, Michael was free to choose plays that inspired him or the directors that worked for him. However, when programming for the theatre, he would also ask himself a series of questions: does the play answer the needs of the theatre? Does it have an unpredictability about it? Does it have something that is fresh? Does it have something that will give the audience an experience they have never had before? Is it good, classy writing? All equally useful and insightful questions when it comes to choosing a play to direct with a young cast. For Michael, choosing a play to direct himself is about gut instinct: "when you get it, it is overwhelming. You think, 'I have to direct this play. I cannot wait to get into the rehearsal room with it'" (Attenborough, 2012). For him, it is also about the text and the language of the play, and how the story can be told to an audience:

> It is a bit like reading a novel. You either want to turn the page or you don't; you either want to get to the end or you don't; you are gripped or you are not gripped. All too often plays are submitted where the texture of the writing is lovely but there is very little at stake. You think, "I am not terribly concerned to get to page twenty when I'm on page two. I admire it but I don't feel compelled by it." Choosing a play is as basic as wanting to read on. (Attenborough, 2012)

Every play choice for Michael was driven by passion and suspense as well as a desire to see how the story unfolds and what happens to the characters in it.

Similarly, for Richard Eyre, choosing a play is not a process – it is instinct: "if I don't respond to it in a first reading, I am never going to respond to it" (Eyre, 2013). Richard believes that the first reading is vitally important for the director – he or she must retain their first impression of the play and value their instinct, because three quarters of the way through rehearsals they will undoubtedly need to recapture that flame that flickered in the first place. Richard's approach to choosing a play has remained consistent, both as Artistic Director of the National Theatre (1987–97) and as freelance director. He believes that the idea of balancing the repertoire with popular plays in order to find time to do the riskier plays is cynical:

> I find that an absolutely contemptible attitude because it despises the audience. If you do not respect your audience then you should not be doing theatre, because without an audience it does not mean anything. Whether you are choosing work to do yourself or choosing shows that are going to go on in a theatre, you have got to act in good faith and you have got to have a clear conscience; you have got to be able to formulate your defence or your desire to do a piece of work. (Eyre, 2013)

As a director of young people, it is important to find a play that both you, and the young people that you work with, can enjoy and connect with – or at least learn to enjoy and connect with over time. The process of putting on a play, whether with a professional cast or with young people, is time consuming and intense. As Richard says, "it is a chunk out of your life," (Eyre, 2013) and, for this reason alone, you must make the right choice.

Director Matthew Dunster approached Michael Attenborough to direct *Before the Party*, by Rodney Ackland, at the Almeida Theatre. As a freelance director, Matthew is not bound by a building or specific audience when choosing a play. However, he still has to pitch that play to a venue and its Artistic Leadership team, and so he has to think carefully about his choice. For Matthew, it is a matter of stretching himself professionally, and not being defined as a certain type of director: "I am always looking to do something that people wouldn't expect me to do. Michael [Attenborough] was very surprised when I took a dry, middle class comedy to him. I have a little private rule for myself, which is to never come out of the same foxhole twice, whether that be as a writer or a director" (Dunster, 2012). He is not interested in having a specific vocabulary, or distinctive identity in the work that he makes, but would rather just "direct a variety of plays and figure out how to do each play and what idea it needs as it comes along" (Dunster, 2012). As a director of young people, it is common to put the learning needs of the participants above your own artistic needs. Whilst this is commendable, after all the learning experience for the young people should be paramount, it is also important to remember why you are doing this and what your role is. Indeed, it is important to heed Matthew's advice and direct something that pushes you and makes you take risks too, because in doing so, you will push the young people involved and encourage them to also take risks.

Whether a director has total freedom to choose a play, is bound by an artistic ethos or audience need, or has a play thrust upon them, it is never an easy choice. Even with freedom comes other considerations – has it been done before? If so, where? And how recently? How many cast members are there and what is the budget? Equally, choosing a play to direct with a cast of young people is not a straightforward task. There is some freedom for personal choice, but there are numerous additional considerations to take into account, like size of cast, gender balance, number of main parts, content and language appropriateness and curriculum restrictions, to name just a few. The questions below will help to filter your choices.

## Questions to ask yourself before choosing a play

### Why are you putting the play on?

Are you directing a youth theatre play or is it a school play? Or is it a play for examination purposes? Your reason for putting the play on will help you to make your play choice. For example, if it is a school play, you will probably want to choose a play with a large cast and also work with other departments to put the play on, so a musical could be more appropriate than a straight play as it will allow you to work with more people, across departments. If you are directing a play for youth theatre, you might want to consider what plays the group have performed before. You might also want to consider something that challenges them – after all, these young people are making an extra, out-of-school commitment to theatre, so you want to take them beyond the school experience. Might a classic text stretch them more than a contemporary piece, for example? The age range of the group will also factor in your decision – indeed, should it be a play written especially for young performers or for a mixed age-range? If you are choosing a play to direct for examination, then there may also be other considerations like the duration of the play, or extract of the play, and the number of actors performing. Choosing a play is a daunting task, but your decision might be made easier by considering why you are putting it on in the first place.

## Who is the play for?

It is important to know your audience. Is the play intended for the friends and family of the cast? Is it for the rest of the school or youth group? Is it to entertain or celebrate, or is there a particular agenda or educational rationale behind the choice? Understanding and respecting the community where you are directing is critical. Specifically in schools, for example, the expectations from the school administration, the school community and the parents needs to be understood and taken into consideration when choosing a play. Dramatic work that is perceived as fine in one community may prompt questions in another – so it may be important to involve the school's administration, or parents, into your decision making process.

## How many actors will you have?

You may be in a luxurious position where you can choose the play first and then cast it, so the play itself dictates this. However, if you are working in a school or community setting where the class or group size is set, and where you have an inclusive policy that allows all young people to participate, regardless of ability or numbers, then you will need to decide if you are going to choose a play that has a large enough cast, or a play with a flexible cast, or even a play where you can add actors in as extras or a chorus when and where necessary. The former approach is tricky as it is pretty difficult to find plays with large casts, let alone the exact number of roles and the correct gender balance for your particular group. If you decide to go down this route, however, there are a number of published playtexts written specifically for young people to perform, for example National Theatre Connections plays, as well as unpublished ones like the Almeida Theatre LAB plays. The former are a mix of large cast plays and smaller casts, whereas the LAB plays have casts of over 15 young people. Both are sources of excellent plays written by high calibre writers. The Theatre for Young Audiences website (www.tya-uk.org) is also a great resource as it lists upcoming UK shows for young people. Whilst these are only aimed at children up to 11 years old, it at least gives you an idea of the organisations who are committed to creating work for young people, who may well also create work for those older than 11. You could also search for plays, according to cast size and male/female ratio, which have been written, adapted or translated, into English since the production of Osborne's' *Look Back in Anger* in 1956 on www.doollee.com. Although this will obviously require a great deal of reading if you do not already know the listed plays. It is also a good idea to see what other people are doing, or have done in the past – would that be suitable for your group too?

It is arguably easier to choose your play based on a flexible cast approach, or a play that can include extras, with large crowd scenes, or a chorus. A flexible cast approach has two options: to split the bigger roles so that a number of young people play one character over the course of the play; or to have different people play the roles on different nights of the run. Both of these options require additional consideration: will the audience accept a character that is played by multiple actors, and if so, how will this affect the overall reception of the play by the audience? And are there enough performances to make it a worthwhile experience for the young actors who perform every other night, and what impact does this have on the rest of the cast, who essentially have to learn to play the piece twice? Neither option is impossible; they just need careful consideration and a well-planned rehearsal schedule. Choosing a play with lots of crowd scenes has its benefits, but the director will need to consider how to engage and motivate his or her extras, so that they do not feel like spare parts. Plays with a chorus are a good option, as although the chorus can be seen as merely an extra, they actually drive the narrative forward, the lines can be split amongst the actors, and there are no limits to how many actors you use. There is also a great deal of potential to be creative and quite physical with chorus work. The difficulty lies in finding plays, other than Greek plays, that utilise a chorus, or something similar. Some musicals utilise a chorus – for example Elle's sorority sisters in *Legally Blonde* and the girls in *Little Shop of Horrors*. The use of the group chorus was also revived in Eugene O'Neill's *Mourning Becomes Electra* and T.S. Eliot's *Murder in the Cathedral*.

## Who are your actors and what is the gender balance?

Are all of your actors incredibly skilled performers, or do you only have one or two confident and able actors in your group? And even if they are able, can the actors play the breadth of roles in the play of your choice, and do they fit the demographics of the characters (age, gender, etc.). And what about the importance of creating space to build on and develop some of the less able or confident performers? Is there space for them to grow into a role? And are the young people well-behaved and committed? Are they capable of learning the lines for the characters? The kind of characters in the play of your choice need to be considered alongside the young people you are working with. You can always dress a girl up as a boy, if the actor is willing, and you can add a wig, costume and make-up to make a 16 year old look like a 60 year old – but these are artistic choices that need to be carefully thought through – and you need to be happy with them. Look to the professional world for inspiration, and make your choices in an informed way. Phyllida Lloyd's all-female *Julius Caesar* at the Donmar Warehouse, for example, received critical acclaim, and she decided to play it with an entire cast of women because she was unhappy that there were not enough parts in plays for women. Equally, Maria Aberg chose to switch the gender of two roles in her production of *King John* for The Royal Shakespeare Company: the Catholic emissary Pandulph and, more radically, the firebrand Philip Faulconbridge, otherwise known as the Bastard, the child of Richard Lionheart.

## How much time do you have?

How much time you have is of utmost importance in choosing a play. It is crucial that you have enough time to prepare and rehearse the piece. Directors working with young people are unlikely to have the luxury of six full weeks of rehearsal time. They may have a two or three week intensive period over school holidays, or a whole term of one or two after school rehearsals a week, or just timetabled lesson times. Either way, it is not anywhere near as long as the professional director has with a professional cast. Equally, unlike professionals who are being paid to commit to one job, young people will have various conflicts on their time, and so scheduling the rehearsal period can be one of the most challenging parts of the directorial process, and needs to be considered very carefully. How can you make productive use of a rehearsal when your leading lady is absent for a maths exam, or your leading man has a basketball match, for example? It is worth bearing in mind that some scripts are easier to work on than others and so are less time intensive, and this may aid your choice of play. Those with smaller casts are often easier than those with large casts or lots of ensemble work. Straight plays tend to be easier than musicals, and modern plays written for young performers easier than Shakespeare, where the language is tricky and committing it to memory even more difficult. The bottom line is, the more challenging the script, the more time you will need.

### How much money do you have?

It is crucial that you know your budget before choosing a play – the more cast members there are, for example, the more costumes you will need, which pushes up costs. The style of your play also has budgetary implications. A straight play, for example, will cost less to produce than a musical. A contemporary play is also likely to cost less than a period piece, unless you are doing the period piece in modern dress, because the participants might be able to use some of their own clothes for costumes, or you can buy them cheaply from the high street, rather than hiring expensive period outfits. But it is not just costumes that cost money. Many plays will require that you pay for performance rights. The cost of these tends to be less for straight plays than for musicals. To save money, you could choose to produce a play that does not require royalties, like one of Shakespeare's plays or a Greek tragedy. These plays tend to be older and are often available online. Alternatively you could commission a writer to write you a new play – this will have cost implications too, but it will be your play and you will present the world premiere of it. Another option is to devise the play yourself with your participants – but this has further time and dramaturgical implications to consider. See Chapter 9.

## What resources do you have?

Before deciding on a play, it is important to think about where it will be performed. What is the venue like? Is it a big auditorium that needs filling with spectacle or a large set, or a small intimate one? And what about the stage? Does it reflect the auditorium size? And what kind of stage is it? Proscenium Arch? Thrust? In the Round? Is it even taking place in a theatre? You also need to consider the technical capabilities of the space, specifically lighting and sound. And if the play needs a lot of technical support, do you have the appropriate designers and technicians available to you? You also need to consider your rehearsal space. Do you have to share the space that you are using with others? If so, is a play with lots of set, costume and props a sensible choice? You will want to get the cast working with these as soon as possible, but may have nowhere to store them, and so you may need to carry them around from space to space with you.

All of the above questions are designed to make you think before you act, and having the answers to these questions (or at least considering them if not) will help to make the process of choosing a play much smoother and enjoyable. It will also enable you to plan effectively – if you know that you do not have a fixed rehearsal space, for example, you know you will need to arrive ten minutes early to a rehearsal to mark up the space each time, and elicit some helpers to transport furniture and props.

So, what next? Commission a writer, get devising or get reading! If you decide that an existing play is the right choice for you and your cast, then you need to get reading. Read, read, read. Then shortlist your favourites and ask yourself all of the above questions again. Choosing the right play from the outset will result in the best possible production – if you love it, that love will rub off on your participants and they will love it too. As Lyndsey Turner says:

> It is pretty tough-going directing a play. So, crucially, pick a play that you love – one that is worth getting out of bed for; one that is worth going back home to a fridge of rotten food for. (Turner, 2012)

The biggest question is how to get passionate about a play if you did not choose it. There is no magic formula for this. Lots of rereading and research will encourage a better understanding of the play, and hopefully the love will follow. Either way, you are putting this production on, and it is now your job to do this as successfully as possible with a group of young people – so good luck!

# 3
# Before Rehearsals Begin

The most difficult task is over: you have chosen the play, new or classic, and now you just need to get started. But what do you need to do before rehearsals begin? This chapter will focus on all of the things that you need to consider before you even enter the rehearsal room. For me, there are five key things on my checklist which include: knowing the play, doing some research, deciding on the physical world of the play, planning the rehearsal schedule, and casting the play. There is not one thing on the checklist that is more important than any of the others. Indeed, all five are crucial, but I will take each of these in turn to interrogate the checklist fully.

## Know the play

It sounds obvious, but it is crucial that you have a detailed understanding and knowledge of the plot and the characters. In fact, I would go as far as to say that one of the most important things to do is make sure that you know your play inside out and back to front. A vague understanding will simply not do. Directors with professional casts can rely on their actors to read the play a few times before they start rehearsals to familiarise themselves with the plot and the characters. Indeed, for Richard Eyre, this is essential pre-rehearsal work for the actor:

> I think it is irresponsible and lazy not to investigate your character. Whether that means thinking about the character, reading things they might read or going to places they might go

to; anything that helps. You are a detective and you are assembling material. (Eyre, 2013)

However, with a young cast, it is far less likely that they will turn up to the first rehearsal having done any preparation, so you may need to factor time into rehearsals to facilitate their understanding of the play and the relationships between the characters. Consequently, you must be absolutely familiar with the play yourself. As Indhu Rubasingham says, "you need to really understand the script. It needs to be in your bones" (Rubasingham, 2012).

The following are some tips for helping to get to know the play, although none can replace the need to read it, and re-read it and re-read it again. However, they will help you to enhance your understanding of it:

### Create a glossary of terms.

Put together a list of words or issues/themes in the play that you think might need defining. There are always words in plays that people do not understand, especially when working with young people, and this will prevent people needing to ask. You can always add to this in rehearsals too.

### Break the play down into its major headlines.

Give each scene a title or a headline that is catchy and sums up the scene. The shorter and snappier they are, the easier they are to remember. You can then use these as shared references for the scenes. You could even do this task with your cast in one of the early rehearsals as this will encourage a sense of ownership and shared understanding of the text. See News Headlines exercise in chapter four.

### Create subheadings for each headline.

This is a little like unit-ing the text – breaking it down into discrete units of action, each marked by a significant change in action. Take each headline and break it into further subheadings – as many as necessary. (I focus on unit-ing in greater detail in chapter five).

### Learn the running order off by heart.

Make flashcards of the titles, scramble them up and re-order them. Once in rehearsals, have your cast do this too. Get them to say them in reverse order out loud and skipping a scene etc. You could do this practically by creating freeze frames too, so that the plot is being considered physically as well as mentally.

**Create character profiles for each of the characters**.

Print pictures of your cast with their character names underneath. Or choose appropriate celebrities to represent them. Again this could be a task that you do with your cast. Ask them if their character was played by a famous person, who would it would be and why? Display these pictures on the wall, in the style of a family tree, if appropriate. If not, use annotated arrows to illustrate the relationships and connections between the characters. Before she begins rehearsals, Indhu Rubasingham takes each character in turn and looks for clues in the play about their personalities – how do they describe themselves? How do other characters describe them? What other facts can you glean from the text about them? Do this yourself first, but you could also have your cast create their roles on the wall, annotating either the picture of themselves, the representative celebrity, or their own drawing with all of their character facets. You could even write them inside the body for internal characteristics and outside for external ones.

If you decide to do some of this work with your cast in the early rehearsals, make sure that you do it yourself first too. There is a great deal of mileage in going on the journey with the young people, but it is equally essential that you have a thorough understanding of the plot and characters yourself. You can still go on that journey with them, you just need to do a dummy run of it first to make sure that everything is fine. There are bound to be things that you missed, or places that you did not have time to visit, which will only make the whole rehearsal process richer.

## Research

Research is a broad term, but it is best to ask yourself what it is that you do not know about this play that is essential to find out before rehearsals begin. Is it set in a different era or culture? Is there a particular angle or theme in the play that you would like to familiarise yourself with? The extent of research that a professional director does varies from director to director and from play to play. If you are working on a piece of new writing, for example, then the best type of research possible is access to the writer – they have already done the research and they know the characters, and you have most likely worked with them from the early stages of script development. When Michael Attenborough directed Neil LaBute's *Reasons to be Pretty*, a play about four people and their interrelationships, he hardly did any research at all:

> All the research I did was talking to Neil really. The great joy of working with a living writer is that, nearly always, if they have written the play well, they talk about the characters as their close and intimate friends. (Attenborough, 2012)

This degree of research will help you to know the play, specifically the characters in the play, and is easy to conduct through conversation. However, unless you commissioned the writer yourself, it is unlikely that you will have the luxury of their presence in rehearsals with you. But if there is a living writer, it may well be possible to get in touch with them and ask them a few questions. Remember, they will be pleased that you have chosen to give life to their play again, and, in my experience, want you to do the best job possible and so will be open to answering a few questions – as long as you are not hounding them! If you really cannot get access to the writer, you could also look at who has directed it before and talk to them; or if it has been produced professionally, there may be online educational resources that provide context for you. Approach this kind of research with caution as nobody wants to see a study guide regurgitated on stage. Just be sure to not let any research restrict your personal interpretation. When I read a play for the first time I do a number of things: I highlight any interesting words or phrases; I make a note of how each scene made me feel after reading it; and I write down anything else that pops into my head, however obscure or seemingly irrelevant – I am often surprised at how many of these immediate, often nonsensical, observations end up featuring in the play somehow. This is a good way to get a first impression of the play and to analyse how you feel about it.

For plays that are set in an entirely different culture to your own, it is important to have a basic understanding of that culture. The degree to which this is possible will vary. For example, when

Michael directed *When the Rain Stops Falling*, by Andrw Bovell, a play by an Australian author set partly in Australia, he visited the country; and when he directed *Filumena* he went to Naples. In contrast, when Indhu directed Lynn Nottage's *Ruined*, which is set in the Democratic Republic of the Congo, she had to rely on books and the internet for her research as the political difficulties in the country meant that she was unable to visit. However, one of the actors in the play was Congolese, which meant that she had an additional source of information: "he could give us really specific gestures and images and could really explain things" (Rubasingham, 2012). Having resources in the rehearsal room that give a sense of the culture of the play is vital, so that you and your cast do not feel totally alien to the world that you are working on. Despite these resources, Indhu, like Mike, would always try if possible to visit the place where the play is set:

> I did a play that was set in Uganda and I got to go out to Uganda. It gave me a different feel for the play, especially as it was about a world and subject that I knew little about. I was able to get a real sense of it. (Rubasingham, 2012)

If it is not possible to visit the locations of the play, or speak to people who have experienced or understand the culture, then you will need to find another way to try to feel something about the play, like finding photos or paintings or poems that can bring that culture to life for you.

If the play that you are working on is set in a different era, then you will probably want to do some research about that era. Some directors choose not to as they believe that the text alone is sufficient, or that that research will emerge naturally through the design of the production. However, when working with young casts, it is likely that, unless they are history students, that you will need to make extra effort to make the period less alien to them. Consequently, you must feel confident that you know and understand the era well yourself. When Richard Eyre is working on a play that is not set in the current time, he will also conduct research into that era, but the extent of the research depends on the period. For his West End production of *Quartermaine's Terms*, by Simon Gray, which is set in the 1960s in a language school in Cambridge, his research was less extensive:

> Coincidentally I happened to be a student at Cambridge at that time, so in theory there was no research to do, except the old saying that if you can remember the 60s then you were not there. However, I found it extraordinarily difficult to remember what people wore – I wore practically what I am wearing now. So research for a play like that would be reading some of Simon's other plays, reading his diaries and looking at photographs of the period. (Eyre, 2013)

Young people, purely because of their age, might not have experienced the era first hand and are consequently only aware of the trends that exist in their own world, so it is essential to create a sense of that time for them. Are there films or photographs or magazines that will help to illustrate the era? A play like Nick Dear's *The Dark Earth and the Light Sky*, set in the early twentieth century and based on the poets Edward Thomas and Robert Frost, has numerous research opportunities because it is based on real people: "you can research the lives of all the people, you can look at photographs of the period, you can read their poems and books, you can read biographies of them, and look at accounts of the period" (Eyre, 2013). For this play, Richard's research was far more extensive.

Some directors will focus primarily on the text itself for research. It is not just about reading it and re-reading it, or knowing it inside out and back to front, but rather about how you read it. As Indhu says:

> You can read the play in different ways. I might read a script to see how many references it makes to the weather or to colour, and I jot that down. Or with characters, I will go through each character and see how they describe themselves and also how other characters describe them. It helps to illuminate the script and open it up in different ways. (Rubasingham, 2012)

Matthew Dunster would echo this sentiment. He is a great believer that the play contains all of the answers and so he focuses primarily on really interrogating the text. For him, the play itself is the most important source of research and any other research is of secondary concern:

> Having been an actor and having been part of the process of "table work," where you sit around and you all read a book about late nineteenth century Russia, I realised it never really did anything for me. I could never wait to get back to the text, and find out what information was in there. (Dunster, 2012)

For Michael, the director is a piece of steak and the text is its marinade: "just letting it soak for a while. Reading it again and again and again and just soaking yourself in it" (Attenborough, 2012). It is vital to know the play well, and a good idea to see what clues it gives you about the world of the play that may then require further investigation.

If the play that you are working on deals with a specific issue or theme that you are unfamiliar with, you will probably want to find out more about this issue or theme. This may seem like a daunting task, but as Indhu says, "when you start researching something or thinking about something, suddenly it is everywhere" (Rubasingham, 2012). Michael would concur: "one of the funny things about research is that you think there have not been any articles about it lately, and then, when you are watching out for it, suddenly there is one every day. They have been there but you have not noticed them" (Attenborough, 2012). There are many sources of research: search the internet, speak to people, read books, find images, and look at pamphlets or guides. You do not need to drown yourself in the research or become an expert; you just need to familiarise yourself with the theme or issue of the play.

One of the key things to remember about research is that it should not be an onerous task, but rather one that inspires you to find out more about the play that you are taking from page to stage. Many directors do their own research, some do it with their casts, some ask their casts to do it independently and some ask their assistants (those who are fortunate to have them) to do it for them, but there is no right or wrong way of doing it. With a young cast though, it is vital that you facilitate their understanding of the play and the world that it inhabits. So, you need to think about how you might disseminate the research and ensure that they have understood it. And if they are doing it themselves, how do you avoid them presenting you with a print out from Wikipedia that is meaningless and undigested? Whenever I work on a text with young casts, I would spend the first few rehearsals, at least, introducing them to the world of the play before even reading it. I will deal more with how to do this in Chapter 4. Despite any research that I had conducted myself, I would approach this period of discovery with them, so that we are all learning together. This is true too for Michael Attenborough, and once he has finished his research, he sticks it in his back pocket:

> The thing to remember about research is that once you have done it, forget it. It is about me, about my person, and I think it sort of seeps into you. I think your response to your research is a kind of fusion between you and the text and the bits of research that bubble at the surface and stay with you are the ones that are the most valuable. And you find that even in the middle of the rehearsal period you suddenly remember that you read something relevant about it, but you had forgotten it and suddenly it comes bubbling up because it is really important. (Attenborough, 2012)

You will be amazed at how something deeply buried can rise to the surface again. You also need to forget your research so that you can be open to your actors – you have to be willing to let go and see what they can bring to the table. It is tempting not to be so open with young casts, but if you want to empower them and avoid "point and shoot" directing, it is vital that you are. Indhu says: "you do the research yourself so that you are confident enough to be open and flexible" (Rubasingham, 2012). This is true of young people too. You need to allow them the space to take ownership of the piece by researching and discovering with you. Indeed, appearing as if you have all of the answers already will be detrimental to any kind of shared experience or journey.

## Decide on the physical world of the play

By this, I am not necessarily talking about an intricate design, but rather the actual locations for all of the scenes in the play and what lies beyond them. You need to know the text

backwards from a physical point of view – the cast will be looking to you to guide them not only in terms of the onstage action
but the geography of what is off stage too. It is a good idea to
walk your actors through the physical journey of the play in early
rehearsals in order to discover any problems with the set; and in
order to do that, you need to be familiar with that journey yourself. As Michael Attenborough says, "you can stare at a model
until you are blue in the face but you do not know if the set is
going to work until you try it" (Attenborough, 2012). And for
most directors of young people, there will not be a model box,
and so having a physical structure in your mind before you go
into rehearsals will help predict any problems and will help you
to consider how the space can help to tell the story. This was particularly true for Indhu when she directed Lynn Nottages's *Ruined*
at the Almeida Theatre in 2010:

> I remember talking to the designer because it is set in many
> different locations – it goes from a bar to a bedroom to out-
> side a bar – and we soon realised that it would be a shame if
> we had to keep stopping the play, stopping the rhythm of the
> play, for a scene change. And so we came up with the concept
> of the revolve. (Rubasingham, 2012)

Equally, when Richard Eyre directed *The Dark Earth and the Light
Sky*, he decided very early on that he wanted to do the play as
simply as possible. He saw a strong visual image – dark earth
and light sky – from which the production emerged. Indeed, the
physical world can be very abstract. Lyndsey Turner is a big fan
of using pictorial references:

> One of the things that I do is to go through huge amounts
> of images that I have collected over the years, selecting those
> which seem to speak to the play. These can be very, very
> abstract and tangential, but they help me to feel my way into
> the world of the play. (Turner, 2012)

If you are fortunate enough to be working with a designer then
they will help you to create this physical world. Your relationship with your designer is important as you need to be able to
trust that they will fully serve the play and you need to be able

to discuss options and be open to suggestions for ideas that you may not have thought of. For Matthew this is a natural process:

> When I work with Anna [Fleischle], who is a designer that I have got a strong relationship with, I say to her, and I *mean* this, "I do not really understand the play until you have designed it for me." Because one of the first things we bring to a play is its relationship with space. How am I going to do it? And where am I going to do it? I feel that in the solutions she puts in front of me, the play is illuminated. I would not have got there myself. (Dunster, 2012)

If you do not have the luxury of a designer, try to find someone else to talk this through with. Better still, find a room big enough to mark out the space and use whatever you can find – chairs, tables etc – to create the physical world. What are the different locations on stage? How and where will the actors enter and exit? You could work through some of these problems with your cast in the early rehearsals if you have time. A good starting point, practically, is to take each of the headings that you invented for getting to know the play. Where are they set? What is their location? Are there any other clues in the text about the physical world of the play? Is it indoors or outdoors? Is there any furniture? What is the landscape? How do the actors enter and exit the space? Can you draw a map of your play for the cast? However you decide to do it, it is important that you have a sense of how you are going to stage the play. Is it in one space or multiple spaces? Do you need to be able to keep the action moving or is it quite static? The more you know about the physical world of the play before the rehearsals begin, the better.

## Planning the rehearsal schedule

Initially, this would be a rough idea of how to break the play down in relation to the amount of rehearsal time that you have. Indeed, the big enemy of the director's time is that there is never enough, whether working with a professional cast or not. However, with a young cast, time is doubly against you. When you break down the number of hours that you have to rehearse, it is likely to produce a final figure in hours rather than days. Lyndsey Turner likes to make a chart of the rehearsal schedule and to develop a rough sense of where she wants to get to by the end of each week. You can easily do the same thing, even if you are only rehearsing one or two evenings a week, by dividing up the sessions and deciding that you want to get to a certain point in the play by a particular session.

Indhu likes to plan her rehearsals in an abstract but structured way:

> Rehearsals are like painting a picture. First there is the rough sketch – getting through the play quickly from beginning to end, because I have a philosophy that it is only when you get through to the end that you know where you have to start. Then I go back to the beginning and it is like adding more colour. And I keep going back over and adding more colour until there is a familiarity and a confidence from the actors. (Rubasingham, 2012)

Even though her schedule is vague, it follows a pattern, and allows her actors to feel secure. Similarly, I like to work in a five-stage process for scheduling purposes, working through the process chronologically and assigning a certain percentage of my overall rehearsal time to each stage, so no matter how much time I have, and whether the rehearsal period is spread over a number of weeks with a few hours each week, or it is an intensive period of consecutive days, I know what percentage of that time I will assign to each stage of the rehearsal process:

### Stage One:

Create the world of the play. Ten per cent of my overall rehearsal period would be given over to this. I would spend time on exercises that focused on understanding, location(s), era, timeframe and culture – everything that gives the play context. I would include the read-through in this stage.

### Stage Two:

Get to know the text – the machine of the play. The next ten per cent of my overall rehearsal period would be dedicated to exploring how all aspects of the play relate to one another, in terms of narrative and characters. What happens? To whom? When? And in what order does it happen?

**Stage Three:**

Get the play on its feet. This is the stage where you test the first hunches of how to do it. Thirty per cent of my rehearsal period would be spent on this stage – how do the young actors inhabit and move around the space? How do they deliver their lines? I would work through the play in order, working out with the actors where they go, what they do and how they do it.

**Stage Four:**

Edit, bring it together and polish. Again, this would utilise 30 per cent of my overall rehearsal period. It is a time to refine things and make decisions. It is time to run scenes together, then acts and then the whole play.

**Stage Five:**

Run it, tech it, dress it. I would spend 20 per cent of my overall rehearsal period on running the show and re-running the show, and then running it once more. This is probably way more time than a professional director would give to a professional cast, but from my experience young people need to know what they are doing and how they are doing it. This will only really be accomplished through running the play. This does not mean that you cannot go back to stage four if necessary for particular moments, but the sooner you get the whole play ingrained in their brains and bodies, the more secure both you and they will feel. I would include the tech and dress rehearsal in this stage too – perhaps not in terms of time, but certainly in terms of thinking.

The following chapters will deal in more detail with each stage, but the idea of the above is to give an idea of how to divide up your overall rehearsal time. So, if I was working with a group of young people over a ten-day intensive period, I would spend one day on stage one, one day on stage two, three days on stage three, three days on stage four and two days on stage five. If I was rehearsing for two-hour sessions once a week for ten weeks, the above days would become sessions. I would then start to layer this with any additional, specific considerations. For example, if there is a fight in the play, when should this be rehearsed? For me, this would fit into stage four. If there are songs or movement, I would want to fit these in as early as possible, prob-ably stage three, but maybe incorporating them into warm-ups for each rehearsal. As Lyndsey says:

> If there are elaborate scenes changes or set pieces, start work-ing on them in week two so that you are not stock piling all the nasty complicated technical jobs for the end of the process where stress is running high and you are getting short of time. (Turner, 2012)

Indhu would concur, because you do not want to panic the actors: "Rehearsals are about making the space and the place as safe as possible so that the actors can explore and take risks but then also feel confident by the time they go on stage" (Rubasingham, 2012). If this is true for professional actors, it is even more per-tinent for young casts – they absolutely must feel confident that they know what they are doing and that they have rehearsed everything enough. Essentially, rehearsals are all about time man-agement. The more you do it, the better at it you will become and the less prescribed you will need to be, like Richard Eyre, who does not plan his rehearsals in a schematic way: "the more expe-rienced you get, the more relaxed you get" (Eyre, 2013). Equally, Michael's system is relaxed, although cerebral:

> After spending day one basically getting everyone together, hopefully blending and enthusing everybody, showing them designs, and talking to them about why I chose the play and how I am planning to do it and so on, I then spend three or four days forensically examining the play, before getting it on its feet. (Attenborough, 2012)

However tightly planned or vague, all professional directors begin with a plan of action. Some systems are planned down to the tiny minutia while others are a bit sketchier, but the director should always know what he or she is doing and when.

## Casting

It sounds obvious, but quite a lot of the above will be made eas-ier if you know who is playing who. For all directors, the most important part of preparation is casting. This is a much trickier area when you are working with young casts for a number of reasons – examination requirements might dictate that all students need to play leading roles, regardless of their performance skills; if you audition students, some may struggle with the rejection of not getting the role that they wanted; there may be a number of skilled performers available to you, but they are not right for the role(s); and/or you may have an inclusive policy where you do not audition. In contrast, the professional director, hiring a professional cast, can simply choose the best person for the role, and not worry about turning someone down. They also often have the assistance of a casting director to help them find the right person for the role. Professional actors should have developed a thick skin, but this is not true of young people, and so if you decide to audition, careful consideration needs to be given to how you conduct auditions and how you inform people about their success.

All directors rely on experience and instinct when making casting decisions. Richard Eyre says, "usually you have a pretty clear idea of a character in your head so that you can see actors, and think they are gifted, but they are not close enough to your notion of the character" (Eyre, 2013). Matthew Dunster's approach is collaborative, but also instinctive: "I am always looking for a group of people that are going to help me do the show. That is different to just casting the right actors for the part" (Dunster, 2012). Indeed, it is as much about how they fit together as how they are as individuals. Similarly, you know your students best. You know how skilled and how committed they are. However, if you are working with a group for the first time, here are a few tips to help you make casting decisions:

### Consider holding workshop auditions.

This will make the actors feel less exposed and, if structured appropriately, will be an opportunity for you to look out for flexible team players as well as skilled performers.

### Remember that some people struggle with sight reading.

If you would like your auditionees to read from the script, consider giving them time to prepare it. Try to give them as much context around the scene as possible. You may have a really gifted actor who is not very good at working out what is happening in the scene independently and so will play it wrong, but on understanding the context could play it perfectly.

**Consider giving the auditionee an improvisation task.**

This will allow you to see how capable they are without a script and will also give you the opportunity to see them interacting with others.

The five pointers on the checklist will equip you nicely for starting rehearsals. It would also be good, when scheduling, to consider your rehearsal space. In a school or youth theatre setting, the space tends to be a shared one and so you have to set up for every rehearsal. If it is possible, try to find a space that can be yours for the duration of rehearsals, that way you can mark up the space, add pictures to the walls, and gather furniture, props and costumes together and leave them there. If this is not possible, you will need to consider how to own the space for each rehearsal and make sure all of the things that you need are portable. The other thing that you might like to consider before you begin is setting your actors tasks. Lyndsey Turner tends to write to a company before she starts rehearsals with them to talk about who else is going to be in the acting company, the makeup of the creative team and how rehearsals are likely to be organised. There is so much anxiety on the first day, so if you can send out some pretty clear signals about what is going on, the more comfortable and confident your cast will be. I always send a character profile to my cast so that they know who they are and what their relationships are to the other characters. I then ask them a few questions for them to complete, like what is your favourite colour, where did you last go on holiday, or what was your first pet? All questions that they can invent the answers to based on their character profiles. I also ask them to find a picture of a celebrity who they think would play their role. Richard Eyre often uses celebrity ideals when describing the kind of actor he is looking for to his casting agent. These character profiles can then be used for some ice-breaker activity in one of the early rehearsals.

# 4

# Stage 1: Create the World of the Play

Now that you know what the play looks like and who will be playing who, it is time to get going. This can be the scary part. This chapter will focus on what to cover in the early rehearsals. It encompasses stage one of the planned rehearsal schedule – creating the world of the play. For me, this is about ten per cent of my overall rehearsal period, but this will differ depending on the complexity of the play. This chapter aims to give you the tools that you need to begin to navigate your way through the play and deal with all of your actors together, in the flesh, in one space. The main aim of the early rehearsals though – whether professional or not – is to ensure that your actors begin to understand the play, and their role within it, and to set up your expectations of the rehearsal process, that is, setting the pace and tone of the rehearsals to come.

However, before embarking on exploring the world of the play, there are two things that need to be considered first: the meet and greet and the read-through.

## The meet and greet

Most professional directors will begin rehearsals with some kind of meet and greet. Everybody involved in the production – cast, creatives, marketing team, technical crew, stage management etc – will all stand in a circle and introduce themselves and tell everyone what their role is in the production. This can sometimes be quite an onerous task, and people barely remember who is who, but it provides a nice opening structure to the first session. Although there will probably be far fewer "other" roles when working with young casts, I always find that it is good to get as many people as possible who are involved in the production to come to the first rehearsal. The art teacher may well be working on the set and props and the cast may not see him or her again until much later in the rehearsal period, but it is good for the cast to see who is who, and for them to understand that much more goes into putting on a play than what is happening in the rehearsal room. You could have some fun with the meet and greet – perhaps play a name game to help break the ice. I often begin by asking people to talk to the person next to them and find out three facts about them (one of the facts must be a surprise – something that nobody else in the room would know or guess about them). I then ask the pairs to present back those facts, on behalf of their partner rather than about themselves, essentially introducing the person that they have just met to the rest of the group. This works whether the cast know each other or not, as the surprise fact adds a new dimension. I sometimes also play a quick game of Truth and Lies. Around the circle, each person tells two truths about themselves and one lie. People can then ask each other at the end of the session which fact was a lie. These games have a dual purpose: they simultaneously introduce people to one another and help to break the ice. A few other name games include:

*Name/Action* In a circle, one at a time, people say their name and do an action (that either expresses the kind of person they are, suggests how they are feeling, or what they like doing). After each person has a turn, the whole group repeats their name and action.

*Point/Walk* Cross the circle, saying someone's name repeatedly until you reach them. The person you are walking towards should then start to say someone else's name and start walking towards them. Keep moving and do not lose energy!

*Name x3* One person is in the middle. He/she needs to say a person's name three times to get them in the middle. However, if that person interjects before the third time by saying their name once, they have failed. Keep trying! What tactics can you use?

**Concentration** Using the following words/actions to set the rhythm and pass names to the beat:

Concentration (pat knees x2, clap hands x2)
Concentration Obligation (pat knees x2, click fingers x2)
Keep the rhythm (pat knees x2, clap hands x2)
Keep the rhythm and the beat! (pat knees x2, click fingers x2)
Name 1 (own name), Name 2 (someone else) (pat knees x2, click fingers x2)
(Then repeat)

It is worth noting that any game that involves rhythm should be played with caution. If you do not know how quickly the group can pick something up, this exercise could be disastrous as rhythm and coordination can be tricky for some. And remember, we are trying to encourage confidence in our cast, not destroy it at the outset, and so choose this game wisely.

**Celebrate the Name** In pairs tell each other as much as possible about your name. Why were you called it? Do you have any nick names? Does it have a meaning? Do you have any stories about your name? Now write a poem about your partner's name. It doesn't need to rhyme or be funny – it just needs to express the essence of that person.

However you decide to run your meet and greet, it is essential that you do something to mark the occasion, after all this is the first time that this group are coming together to put on this play. It is also a good time for the director to say a few words, as she is unlikely to have everyone together in one space at the same time again until they start running the show.

## The read-through

After the meet and greet, most professional directors will conduct a read-through of the play. Some directors believe that reading the play out loud with their cast is crucial – it is a communal experience that allows the play to be heard. Indeed, it is the first time that the play is given life off of the page. Matthew Dunster tells his actors not to feel any necessity to act. For him, this is of paramount importance because it is the only time that we hear the play for the first time; and you can never hear it for the first time again. What he wants, most importantly, is to *hear* the play, and if actors make, what he calls, extreme, brave day-one choices, this will just get in the way of listening to the text. Michael Attenborough would concur. He tells his actors, "above all else do not worry. You are not performing. Let us hear the play" (Attenborough, 2012). Others believe that the read-through is less important. For Indhu, it is just one of the rituals of theatre – an unnecessary evil that merely serves to break the ice. She has experimented with not having a read-through before, but she soon came to realise that, whilst not important for her, they were crucial for her cast as it grounded them and ensured they were all starting from the same place. She always begins with them, even though she does so with reluctance. Michael Attenborough, in contrast, believes that the read-through is of paramount importance. He begins every rehearsal period with one, and the cast and creative team sit around a central table with everyone else sitting in a circle around them. The table is important to Michael – he spends a good deal of the early rehearsals doing 'table work' – sitting with the actors talking through the play and analysing its language. Matthew, in contrast, never sits around a table, as he thinks it is deadly:

> I do sit around in a circle, and that might not sound any different, but to me it is all the difference in the world, because it is democratic, and because you can see everybody – see their knees and see their ankles. If you put apparatus in front of an actor that make them feel safe, then they will just grab on to it. You can literally see table work where people have got hold of the script in one hand, and the table in the other hand; and when you take the table away, it is like you have chopped their legs off. What is interesting about the circle is that people immediately start to play across it, because they can sort of feed off of the other person's body. (Dunster, 2012)

Whether sitting behind a table or not, both Matthew and Michael have great respect for the text. This is the life-blood of the play and needs careful attention. Some directors have the confidence to dispense with the read-through altogether. Michael never does a read-through of a Shakespeare play, as he believes it is daunting and everyone knows what happens anyway; however he would always do a read-through of a new play. Some directors do a read through, but postpone it until the actors have had a chance to get to know one another. Lyndsey Turner often does it towards the end of the first week instead of it being the first thing that they do. It is worth remembering that even some professional actors dislike read-throughs. Richard Eyre believes that the read-through is a necessary evil, and that "all the actors, regardless of age and experience are always very, very nervous. They are thinking 'Oh God. In ten minutes I am going to have to speak these lines in public. Am I the right person for this part? Can I do it?' No good actor approaches a new part without a great deal of self-doubt" (Eyre, 2013). And so if the thought of a read-through terrifies some professional actors, how must it feel for the non-professional teenager?

Deciding on how to deal with the read-through with a young company is difficult. One of the most crucial objectives for putting on a play with young people is securing their buy-in. They must own the text. And in order to own it, they must understand it and love it. The danger of just sitting down to read the play, especially if there are only a few 'main' parts, is that the cast will get bored and fidgety and quickly lose interest. This is not good when you want their buy-in! So how can you make the read-through a genuinely engaging and meaningful experience? And how can you ensure that it serves one of the crucial objectives of the early rehearsals for your actors to understand the world of the play? If you decide on a traditional approach, then sitting in a circle without a table, like Matthew, is best as it at least encourages openness and there is nowhere to hide. It would be wise to have plenty of breaks or even intersperse the read-through with some physical activity – remember, an active mind needs an active body, and activity can eliminate any boredom and fidgeting. However, the best approach to a read-through with a young cast is to make it as active an experience as possible. Below are a number of active read-through exercises to consider. It is worth remembering before embarking on any read-through activity though that not all young people, and this is true of professional actors too, have a good level of sight reading fluency; and a read through can horribly expose individuals in the company who are not as deft at sight reading as others. If you auditioned your cast, or you know them already, you may well be aware of who these people are and so can find a way to work round the problem. If not, giving the cast a copy of the script in advance and warning them that a read-through will happen will ease that anxiety and allow the less competent sight readers time to familiarise themselves with the text. I always offer people the opportunity not to read if they feel uncomfortable doing so, as there will be plenty of others in the cast willing to stand in. Alternatively, I play around with who reads the lines, swapping in and out or going round the circle line by line (although I would not use either of these techniques if I was visually trying to get people to see who is playing who as a means of understanding the play). Whatever you decide to do, the most important thing is to be mindful of this. One of the strategies I also use to cope with a struggling sight reader is to break the play down into scenes, and break the read-through up so that we read a scene then do a game, then read another scene and then do another game, so that we are not presented with an elongated, painful hour or more of one person floundering through every single word on the page.

Each of the exercises listed below can be used for reading the whole play, or you could switch between them for variety or if you need to keep your cast on their toes:

*The Triple Circle* Read each scene at a time, in order. Ask your cast to sit in three circles:

1. An inner circle – this includes all characters who are in the scene, even if they don't speak.
2. A middle circle – this includes any characters who are referenced in the scene, but don't appear in it. NB – if there are characters who are referenced but don't actually appear in the play (maybe there is a mother who lives in Australia for example), then either a cast member without any lines, or a stagehand can sit in as this person (i.e. someone from the outer circle can step in).
3. An outer circle – this is all other characters in the play who are not in this scene and aren't referenced in it.

You are now ready to read the scene. There are three rules:

1. Say your character's name before you say your line.
2. Stand up when you say your line.
3. Stand up when someone else says your name or talks about you.

As the read-through progresses, encourage all cast members to join in and say a character's name when he/she stands to deliver their lines, or if they are referenced. Eventually, everyone will be saying all of the characters' names. The idea is that this read through technique will get the whole cast involved – even if they don't have any lines – and will get them familiar with the other characters in the play and who is playing who.

After reading the first scene, the configuration of the circles will change – based on the characters in, or referenced in, the next scene. This exercise is very much about getting to know the people in the play, and their relationships with each other. You could try a different version of this which encourages fact gathering and questioning – see below.

***The Triple Circle (version 2)*** As above, divide the group into three circles:

1. An inner circle – this includes all characters who appear in the scene, even if they don't speak.
2. A middle circle – the fact gatherers.
3. An outer circle – the questioners.

Now read through the play scene by scene, swapping people in and out of the inner circle as necessary. Make sure that there are enough pens and pieces of paper for everyone in the middle and outer circles. As the inner circle reads through the scene, everyone in the middle circle writes down all of the facts in the scene and everyone in the outer circle writes down any questions that they might have, that is, things that do not get answered in the scene and/or things that might need some research. I recently used this unconventional read-through with MGCfutures Company on a read-though of Martin McDonagh's *The Cripple of Inishmann,* but with the added dimension of asking the inner circle to use **Point and Place** (exercise below), and after each scene I got them up on their feet to do **Read and Repeat** (exercise below). I was genuinely astonished by how well the group grasped the narrative and characters of the play from a first read-through.

***Point and Place*** Have the cast sit in a circle as per a traditional read-through. You should also set up some chairs or tables in the room to represent different places (or referenced characters who don't appear in the play). Now ask the cast to read the play, with the following rules:

1. Point at yourself whenever you talk about your character.
2. Point at any other characters that you talk about.
3. Point at a table or chair in the room if you talk about a place or a character who doesn't appear in the play. Every time this place or character is mentioned, the actor should point to the same place.

Much like Triple Circle, this read-through technique gets the cast familiar with the other characters in the play and who is playing who, but it also gets them to start thinking about location too.

***Read and Repeat*** Read through in the traditional way, taking the play scene by scene (or if there aren't scenes, break it down into manageable sections). At the end of each scene, ask the cast to repeat the scene in the style of an Italian run-through (i.e. using their own words, and with speed). Alternatively, you could repeat using the following three stage process:

1. Have the students paraphrase the scene.
2. Repeat again, but this time reduce the paraphrasing to a single word.
3. Repeat again, but this time reduce the single word to a single action (for example, instead of saying help, they clasp their hands together in prayer).

Both the Italian run-through and the three stage process can either be done sitting or upon their feet. The purpose of this exercise is to ensure that the company understand what they are reading as they are asked to repeat it in their own words. It also means that they need to use their brains to recall the events of the scene and are active in between scenes.

*The Play Reading Quiz* Read through one scene at a time. After each scene hold a quick quiz. Divide the cast into small groups of three or four people, and encourage them to come up with their own team names and response sounds – extra points should be rewarded for making them thematically linked to the play. You are the quiz master. It might be an idea to appoint an assistant too who can keep tally of the score. Now ask a series of questions relating to the scene they have just read. This exercise requires additional preparation by you – in the form of questions – but it encourages competitiveness and team spirit, and means that all members of the cast are required to actively listen to the scene in order to do well in the quiz.

It is up to you whether you decide to do a read-through or not, and if so, when you will do it. However, there is clearly some value in hearing the play aloud and using this as an opportunity to ensure that your students understand the text; that they agree about what it means, what the important events are, and who the characters are and how they are related to one another. All of the above exercises will also go some way to alleviating any anxieties about both the read-through and the rehearsal process. They are not only a means for introducing the play, and understanding it better, they also double up as ice-breakers as they encourage movement, discussion and active participation, leaving little room to be afraid. As Richard says, "You have got to start somewhere and it is a way of laying out the manifesto" (Eyre, 2013). I agree with Richard. For me, a read-through with a young cast requires preparation. I would definitely do one, but not in the first rehearsal, as there are other, gentler ways to introduce the text that can double up as excellent ice-breakers and help the company to gel.

Once you have completed the meet and greet and read, or not read, through the play, you must now consider how your cast will create the world of the play and get to know the text a little better.

## Creating the world of the play

Part of creating the world of the play is about fostering good group dynamics. And for me, this starts with ice-breakers. Indhu says:

> The most important thing is that you get their [the actors'] trust, and that they trust that you are taking them on the right journey; that is more important than a read through. How do you get their trust by making them feel safe? Making them feel heard? Being clear yourself? Having quite clear boundaries? (Rubasingham, 2012)

That trust and buy-in is especially crucial with a young cast. I always make my ice-breakers thematically linked to the play as a route into the text so that the cast can embody the world of the play before they have even read it. Below are a few suggested, pre-read-through exercises that simultaneously encourage team work and give an introduction to the world of the play:

*The Whoosh!* This requires a little preparation by you. Write your own narrative version of the play, taking care to include the key parts of the story, and all of the characters, including extras. Every time there is a change of scene or time or location, mark it in the story. This will become a whoosh. Have the group sit in a circle. Read the story aloud, and pull actors up into the middle of the circle to create images of the scene – they can be both characters and inanimate objects. You may also want to feed the characters' lines, or ask the objects to make appropriate sounds. When you reach a whoosh, all of the actors must sit back down and you will bring up new ones to tell the next bit of the story. Work your way around the circle as many times as you need to until the entire story has been told. By listening to the story and getting it up on its feet, the cast will begin to get an understanding of the plot and characters in the play. They will gain an understanding of the structure of the piece – how many scenes there are, how they follow on from each other, how many actors are in each scene etc. They will also have to start thinking of the physical world of the play – where are the scenes taking place? What scenery is there? What is the atmosphere like? Etc.

***News Headlines*** Give your cast ten sentences or plot points from the play; these may or may not be dictated by the breakdown of the scenes, all on separate pieces of card (you could do this in smaller groups of five or six, depending on size of cast). First, have them sequence the cards in chronological order and discuss. It may be that your play does not follow chronological order, but the cast has sequenced them chronologically – this is then a great way to start a conversation about the structure of the play and its timeline. Once they have sequenced the sentences, have them turn them into front page news headlines. You could ask them what makes a good headline? Playing on words, alliteration, short and punchy etc. You could also extend this by asking them to create freeze frames, in ten seconds, as you call out the headlines – again this is great for group dynamics as the cast have to work together quickly and creatively in the moment. In this exercise the cast are learning about the plot of the play, they are working together to consider its structure and they are responding to it creatively. You could even use these new headlines to replace some of the ones that you devised before rehearsals began to get to know the play. Or this exercise could be extended for the benefit of creating these collectively.

***Anyone Who*** Get the group to sit in a circle, on chairs, with one person in the middle whose aim it is to sit down. They make a statement that is true to themselves e.g. anyone who ate breakfast this morning … All those for whom the statement is true, must change chairs, including the person in the middle (although people are not allowed to move to the chair next to them). Whoever is left without a chair must now go into the centre and make a new statement. Cast members could start to introduce statements about the play and/or their feelings and thoughts about the play. This game is great for people to loosen up and see what they have in common with other cast members, but it is also a great way of gaging people's feelings about the play.

***Numbers*** Ask the group to move around the space. When you say a number, they must get into a group of that number – with different people each time. You could also add a body part to that number, and the body part must be touching, e.g. five, knees! Equally, once in groups, you could have them create images or scenes from the play in a five or ten second time limit. They could even create physical landscapes or places to help understand the locations in the play. Get them to add sounds to illustrate the atmosphere or mood of the images. This warm-up is a really quick ice-breaker and is particularly good if there are some trust issues in the group or they need to overcome fear of close contact. It is also good to create random groupings before further work.

***Machines*** Take a theme or idea from the play and create a whole-group machine to suggest that theme or idea using actions and sounds. Encourage people to connect and work together – can they add to or build on somebody else's action? Slow the machine down. Speed the machine up. This is particularly good if the play is set in a different era or culture as students can discuss afterwards how the machine suggested a different time or place to the one that they currently inhabit.

Once we have established a little bit of the world of the play, I would then do a read-through, but not a traditional one, and then we are ready to move to stage two of the rehearsal process and start to interrogate the play further.

# 5
## Stage 2: Get to Know the Text

Once everyone knows each other and they have a sense of the world of the play, it is time to really focus on getting to know the text – the machine of the play. This chapter focuses on how to fully acquaint your cast with the play.

Many directors spend a good week on table work, where they discuss the play in detail, ensuring that they understand it, the characters in it and the world that they are trying to create. They spend time interrogating the play in order to fully understand and interpret it, establishing the key facts and often finding answers to, thus making decisions about, things that are not written in the text. Additionally, it is highly likely that the actors themselves would have done some preparation before rehearsals begin – they would certainly have read the play a few times, if nothing else, and they would probably have done a bit of work thinking about their character, and even some research around the subject if they are not familiar with it. Richard Eyre notes that, even though he does not ask them to, "good actors will take it upon themselves to research bits of the play that they do not understand or look on the internet to start getting into the imaginative world of the play" (Eyre, 2013). Michael Attenborough tries to persuade his actors not to research before rehearsals too much. Occasionally, he will send an actor a book or refer them to a relevant television programme, but he firmly believes that, "one of the jobs for a director is not just to research, but also to decide what research is important for the actors" (Attenborough, 2012). It is his job to guide his actors and point them to appropriate research, for example when directing Margo Leicester as the mum in *The Knot of the Heart*, by David Eldridge, he guided her to certain bits of factual, written research before showing her some videos, "that were absolutely gut wrenching; and she said, 'last week you opened our brains this week you have opened our hearts.' And that is exactly what I was doing, and I was doing it in a very particular order" (Attenborough, 2012). Similarly, when working with young casts, you will need to guide their research.

The youth theatre director, in contrast to the professional director, does not have the luxury of a week of round the table analysis – nor, in a majority of cases, would the cast have the attention span for it – so the director of young casts needs quick and easy ways into text and characters. Equally, it is unlikely that his/her cast would have done any preparation before the start of rehearsals. Even if they had been asked to read the play, which many committed and astute young people would do, it is highly unlikely that they will have formulated a list of questions about it, or have conducted any additional research. It is much more likely that they would have counted the number of lines that they have, or skimmed the piece only once.

The youth theatre director is also working within a significantly reduced time frame compared to the professional director. Rather than three to five weeks rehearsal time, they are usually meeting for two or three hours a week. Rehearsal hours in professional theatre are usually 10am to 6pm with an hour for lunch and scheduled tea breaks in the morning and afternoon – well over 100 hours of rehearsal time, depending on the run. Interestingly, the British rehearsal period is pretty short in comparison to other countries; so what must they think about the fact that a youth theatre group are likely to have rehearsed for the grand total of week, if that, when all of their weekly rehearsals are added together? Not to mention the fact that this week is a fractured week – interspersed with the grind of daily life – school, college, work, friends, relationships etc. The professional actor has the evening off with barely time to immerse him/herself in the real world; whereas the young cast has entirely the opposite experience where a majority of his or her time is spent in the real world with only a few hours a week to get back into the world of the play. This is particularly challenging for the director of young casts as momentum is lost from week to week, and time has to be spent at the beginning of each rehearsal on recapturing and remembering, eating even further into a precious and finite rehearsal period.

So how do you begin to get your cast to understand the play, and what you intend to do with it, without table work? Teachers have often said to me that they struggle to have an overall vision or idea for the play, and even if they have one, they struggle with communicating it. However, Richard would not be concerned by this – he believes that a vision is something to be wary of as it sounds very much like conceptual art in that you start with an idea of the play and you then pummel the play and the performance to fit your idea:

> If you start off with the production wholly conceived, then you just slot the actors into your conception. That works fine in theory, and occasionally you see productions that look very good at the model stage, where the theory is immaculate; but if it does not have a life of its own on stage, there is no point. It is just wasting everybody's time ... I work the opposite way. I might have an idea of the architecture of the play, and have a sense of the landscape, but actually the building is something that happens in rehearsals and the actors are the builders. You are assisting them. The director is not going to appear on stage, so you are conducting, assisting, and enabling the actors to arrive at a collective vision. (Eyre, 2013)

Richard has a framework – a piece of architecture, where the building blocks are up for negotiation; and the key thing for him is to invite the actors into the imaginative world of the play in order to discover the vision collectively. Similarly, Indhu takes the analogy of thinking of a play in terms of a piece of music: "you need to know how it starts, where it is going to build, and how and where it is going to either speed up or slow down. You need to think of it very much rhythmically. All of the characters journeys are different instrumental parts to a symphony" (Rubasingham, 2012).

Lyndsey Turner likes to build the imaginative world fairly early on in the rehearsal process. The company will go through the play together noting everything in the play that is an absolute fact, and then asking questions to clarify those facts:

> For example, in a time of war: how long has the war been going on? Who is winning? What is the impact of that war on the population? What is morale like within the soldiers' camp? (Turner, 2012)

She does not attempt to answer these questions during the early rehearsals, she is merely interested in encouraging the company to ask them. She believes that a question asked in one area of the play might help to answer a question in another area of the play. Eventually all of the questions will get answered in a way that makes the most exciting choice possible from an actor's perspective:

> So for instance if you are asking, "what is the morale like inside the soldiers' camp" and your answer is, "fine," you have not got as much to play with as if you say, "morale is really, really low." (Turner, 2012)

For Lyndsey, constant questioning enables a better understanding of the play. This notion of questioning is useful with young casts too. It fosters the idea of enquiry. I always tell my cast that no question is too silly, so that questioning can easily become a natural part of the process. It also keeps the cast on their toes – if they are constantly questioning, they are constantly thinking about the play – which is useful during any big breaks between rehearsals. Matthew feels it is important to keep his actors aware of the play as a whole by re-reading and re-reading:

> What happens is you forget the context of the whole play. Because you read it on the first day, then everybody starts unit-ing, and then you rehearse those units; and then a million years later – week four or five – you start to put it back together again. (Dunster, 2012)

When Matthew has roughly staged act one, he will re-read act two before starting to stage it, "just so that the actors are constantly aware of what their whole arc is. Because you can get to the end of the play and realise that the work you have done on act one scene one is a waste of time" (Dunster, 2012). This would be useful for young casts too. Perhaps not re-reading, but certainly revisiting exercises like the whoosh or news headlines.

Matthew also likes to use improvisation to help create the world of the play. Many professional directors do not veer from the text, and the idea of improvisation is alien to them. But for Matthew it deepens the actors' understanding of the world they inhabit. And he always leaves the room when he sets up an improvisation:

> I say I will be back in 45 minutes and I want to see it. If I am in the room and I am observing what they are trying to do, then I am complicit with what they think the end product should be; and I am not as good an objective judge. So I will come back in and watch it, and tell them what I do not understand or what was brilliant or enlightening. If I had heard little snippets of conversation, and seen them try something that failed and then trying again; and it nearly worked but not really, I would watch what they were presenting to me and think it worked because I had witnessed the process – I would have heard them say it was a baby in a pram, so I would know it was a baby in a pram. (Dunster, 2012)

By leaving the room, Matthew can be incredibly clear-eyed and objective about what he is watching. This can also be useful when working with young casts too, as long as they are motivated to continue to work when you are not present, as just by standing back you are providing the space and freedom that has the potential to yield creative results. Below are a series of exercises to help your students understand the text in greater depth, specifically what happens in it and to establish its key facts. This will enable your students to have a more sophisticated understanding of the play:

*Create the landscape of the play* First, divide the group in half and give each group alternate scenes in the play and ask them to create the actual physical landscape of the piece, one scene at a time, using their bodies and sounds to animate it. Take a photo of this and display it on the wall. Perform these back to each other. What words or feelings does each scene evoke? Make a list of these words.

Once you have the photos, extend the above task by creating mood boards for each scene. Bring in newspapers, magazines and colour charts. Ask the group to place the photo in the centre and then create a collage around it to represent the physical world of each scene. This can be literal or conceptual, or both. Now annotate it with the list of words that were generated. Now put these collages on the wall as a visual reminder.

You could also extend this exercise by either playing the scene in front of the landscape, or paraphrasing it – so that the text is aligned more fully with the landscape of the piece.

***Bring the landscape to life with improvisation*** Give the students time to bring the physical landscape to life. What happens in that space before and after the scene? Is it inhabited by people who do not actually appear in the play, a busy town or market place for example? Maybe follow Matthew Dunster's advice and leave the room to see if you fully understand the world the students are creating. And if not, why not? What could they do differently to make it clear?

***Get on the train!*** This exercise is a precursor to unit-ing the play. Essentially it asks students to explore the rhythmic and/ or emotional journey of the piece:

1. Ask students to identify the stations on the journey – that is, to pick the pivotal moments or key events in the play.
2. Is the train travelling up hill, downhill or on the flat between stations? And how steep are the hills?
3. Have them decide what speed the train is travelling between each stop.
4. Now have your students move from one side of the room to the other, stopping at the stops and adjusting their speed and movement depending on the altitude of the terrain and speed of the train, ultimately representing the rhythmic/emotional journey of the play.

5. Share and discuss these journeys – and make a collective decision about the most truthful journey as you see it at the beginning of the rehearsal period.

This does not mean that the journey should now remain fixed. As Michael Attenborough says, 'If you have completed the exercise and you think you have arrived at a solution to something then you have probably limited the amount you might have travelled. So it is well to keep the journey going' (Attenborough, 2012). As you embark on the rehearsal period, and travel further on that journey, you will discover new key moments that may well take your journey in an altogether different direction.

*One minute story* This exercise helps with understanding of character:

1. Have students go through the play and list all of the things that their characters say about themselves, or other characters say about them. Be careful to distinguish between fact and fiction.
2. Now look at the lists – what kind of person is your character? What do you know about him/her?
3. In pairs, speak about yourself (in character) for one minute. Then swap.
4. Pairs should then introduce their partner's character to the rest of the group. This encourages cast members to understand each other's' characters as well as their own.

If you have a large number of extra characters or chorus members, this is still a great exercise – they just get to be a little more imaginative. If they are playing a man in a crowd scene, then they should invent a life for that man. Who is he? Who are his family? What does he do for a living? Why is he there? This will help them to create more rounded crowd characters, which will, in turn, help when directing the crowd scenes – the characters will have purpose rather than just walking on and off for no apparent reason.

**Parallels** Ask your cast to look for parallels between their own lives, and the world around them, and the play. Richard Eyre said, "plays are almost all about extremes of behaviours and extremes of emotion and you have to create an atmosphere in rehearsals where people can freely talk about their own lives without feeling that they are in confession and without feeling that their account of their lives is going to be betrayed." You might like to have them create a storyboard of parallel worlds/experiences so that these can be drawn upon later in rehearsals.

**Monologue exercise** This is really a dramaturgical exercise that enables a deeper understanding of character. Each cast member should write a monologue for their character in the play, set in their back stories:

1. Read the play twice – once to understand the plot, and a second time to examine the text more closely, making notes about everything you discover about your character – their history, temperament, motivation etc (look for clues in what the writer says about the character, what he/she says about him/herself and what other characters say about him/her). If you prefer you can draw an outline of your character and annotate it – noting all of the internal characteristics inside the body and the external ones outside.
2. Think carefully about how these facets/character components can be demonstrated to an audience.
3. Write a monologue (two to three minutes in length) for your character set a year before the play. Try to mirror the spirit of the original writing. Check against your list of facets – does your monologue manifest at least three of these? Be as specific as possible to the character's experience/feelings at the moment you have chosen. Do not attempt to give an entire back story or cover all of their current circumstances. It is far better to react to an incident, experience an emotion, or have a conversation with someone, rather than relating detailed narrative/telling a story from the past. The most effective way of thinking about writing the monologue is to create a whole scene, in your

imagination, in which the action/dialogue has reached a point where your character needs to speak for two to three minutes, remembering that the other character(s) in the scene are entirely your own invention and NOT other characters in the play.

4. Prepare this monologue, fully learnt, for performance.

Once your actors fully understand the play, and their role within it, you are almost ready to begin getting the text on its feet. However, there is one further thing that I consider crucial to the early rehearsals – in fact, I would do this in the very first rehearsal – and that is to set up a contract of behaviour that fully sets up expectations before rehearsals begin.

## Contracts

For me, contracting a young company is vital. It should be a two-way contract that is agreed collectively. It should also be recorded – in photographs, on a poster, on a graffiti wall – so that it is a constant point of reference. If cast members are reneging the contract, then it is there as a reminder, as something that they signed up to, that will help you to get them back on track. Finally – it needs to be realistic – otherwise you will have a cast of renegers. Creating a contract together can be as simple as collectively writing a list that everyone signs, although I prefer to be more creative in setting up a contract as it makes a pretty dull task a little more interesting and therefore more memorable. Below are a few ideas for creating contracts:

*Freeze Frames* Split the cast into groups. Have each group come up with three freeze frames to illustrate three different rules. Share back and discuss. Take photographs to record. These should also be used as a point of discussion. Is there anything that is missing? If so, give the whole group the count of ten to create another freeze frame to illustrate it. Again, photograph and record.

*Traffic Lights* Put a large picture of some traffic lights on the wall. Red means things that you SHOULD NOT do – be late, talk when others are talking etc. Amber means things that you can SOMETIMES DO – this usually includes things like swearing, chewing and fighting if they are in the play, for example. Green means things that you should ALWAYS DO – turn up on time, be prepared etc. Have students come up one at a time and annotate the traffic lights with rules. Make sure everyone is in agreement before committing to paper. This then provides a visually interesting contract for display purposes.

*Samurai* This is actually a game, but I like to play it with the cast and then ask them to consider how the skills necessary for playing this game effectively translate to us working together to put on a play – things like team work, cooperation, taking responsibility, rules etc. It is a game of attack and defence. Two teams battle it out using five samurai moves (you can make these up but they should be whole body gestures). The team leader makes an attack move, and everyone else in the opposing team, including the leader, responds with an appropriate defence move. After the move, they come back to a neutral position. The other team leader now makes an attack and the opposing team defend. The play continues with team leaders taking it in turns to attack. If people make the wrong move then they are out, but when they are out they still have a role to play – praying to the Samurai God for forgiveness. If they fail to play their part when they are out then another member of their team will suffer by being pulled out too!

You now have your cast fully prepared and they have entered into a contract of agreement – so now it is time to really get started and properly lift the play from the page. It is time for stage three of the rehearsal process.

# 6
# Stage 3: Getting the Play on Its Feet

You have now spent some time getting to know the play, specifically the characters and the story, but what do you do now with lots of words on a page? And how to you turn those words into a performance? This chapter will focus on four simple steps to getting the play off the page and onto its feet: unit-ing, action-ing, blocking and off-text work.

## Unit-ing

To begin with, most professional directors do something called unit-ing the play, which basically means that they break it down into bite size chunks, or units. Units, also sometimes called beats, were first suggested by Konstantin Stanislavski as a means of helping actors determine the through line or super objective of a role; that is the overarching desire that drives him/her through the play. A unit is a discrete piece of action in a play-text, marked by a significant change in action. Most plays easily break down into sections, whether it is scenes or acts, which can then be split up even further so that each new entrance, or even a change in atmosphere or subject, marks a new unit of action. Some directors will have broken the play down into these units before rehearsals begin, but others will work on unit-ing with the actors. Lyndsey likes to divide the play up into smaller chunks with the actors because, "what you are doing at that moment in rehearsals is agreeing on a proposition of the architecture of the play. The highs, the lows, the topography, the landscape. Where are the peaks, the valleys and the cliffs?" (Turner, 2012). Michael Attenborough talks about units as if he is driving a car. He looks for "gear changes, from first, to second, to third. It is actually looking for the way in which the vehicle goes through a gear change" (Attenborough, 2012). Something happens that kicks the play into a different direction: "are we suddenly going into third gear here? And now is it cruise control?" (Attenborough, 2012). The use of an analogy is particularly important for Michael, as actors can often try to present every facet of their character within the first two or three scenes. He has to convince them to reveal their character like an onion, peeling away layer after layer. Plotting through the play carefully, unit by unit, will help to achieve this.

Once the play is broken down into bite sized chunks, directors will begin to work on these chunks, one at a time, to try to understand them and get through the play. They start working on little chunks and then begin to let the chunks get bigger and bigger. For Indhu, unit-ing is akin to learning a piece of music:

> You might learn one line of music, followed by the next line, and then you might put the first two lines together to make sure that the join flows. If it doesn't, why doesn't it? Does that mean you have to change the way you play the first line in order to get to the end of the second line? (Rubasingham, 2012)

The musician keeps on working this way until he or she reaches the end of the piece of music. Equally, Indhu works through the play, unit by unit, scene by scene, until she reaches the end. Indeed, for the professional director, the unit is like a skeleton, and you are adding the flesh, layer by layer. So when a director starts working on a unit, they are stopping all of the time, trying different things, talking about every single word. They are discovering what is working in the scene and what is not, and finding solutions to those problems. A play is a very different animal once you attempt to get it on its feet and once there are lots of people working on it. Things that you thought might work in your head suddenly reveal themselves in a different way, often a much better way. Matthew Dunster firmly believes that it is crucial to work through scenes with the actors, solving any problems that arise collectively. When he was an actor, he wanted everything to be solved in the room and so he wants to honour the actors in his process by making them part of the solution finding and decision making. He says:

> You should never ignore an actor who says, "I don't feel comfortable in that beat," or, "I don't know what I'm doing here." Even if you think that they are being precious, or trying to buy time for themselves, you ignore those frustrations at your peril. (Dunster, 2012)

Working in such microscopic detail is exciting to professional actors – for many it is the highlight of the rehearsal process – but it can be problematic with young casts, particularly if you have lots of other cast members sitting around and getting fidgety. Equally, unit-ing with an untrained cast, rather than for them, is not quite as straightforward as it requires a great deal of concentration and discussion. However, despite this, it is well worth attempting to unit with your young cast as it will give them far greater ownership and understanding of the play.

So how can you approach unit-ing with young casts? I would definitely break the play down for them, but I would help them to take ownership of those units by asking them to give each one a headline or title. Again, see the News Headlines exercise in Chapter 4. This will help with their understanding of the unit, but will also help with scheduling. For example, saying, "today we are working on The Lovers' Quarrel" rather than "Act three, scene two" is far more meaningful. This is something that both Richard Eyre and Matthew Dunster do with their actors, although Matthew does not do it for every scene: "I will only title it if I think people do not understand what they are doing" (Dunster, 2012). If you do want to unit with your cast, then you could approach this by dividing the cast into smaller groups, taking a scene each, and ask them to present that scene in pictures – each picture must signal a shift in atmosphere or mood – a "gear change." They will then determine how many pictures, and ultimately units, the scene has. Alternatively, you could incorporate unit-ing into the read-through, particularly if you have a large cast with only a few speaking roles, and you want everyone to engage with the text. You could ask non-speakers to stand or move every time they notice a gear change, and have someone note these changes in the text.

## Action-ing

Now that you have unit-ed, you need to consider how to work through each unit in microscopic detail. How can you ensure that your young cast understand what is happening and that they understand the language and what their character means when he or she says a line? Matthew Dunster sometimes uses a technique devised by Max Stafford Clark called action-ing which involves breaking the text into sections, and the actor has to find a transitive verb to accompany each individual action. So even the simplest line, like "how are you?" will be attributed an appropriate transitive verb – is it greeting, enticing, seducing, for example? This is also a useful exercise to use with young people, helping them to grasp the meaning of a line and/or making decisions about how to play it if the meaning is ambiguous. It would also be useful to create a glossary of terms to put on the wall. At the beginning of any rehearsal process when working with young casts, I always put two large pieces of paper on the wall. One is for any questions that might arise, remembering to establish the fact that no question is too stupid by putting the first one up myself; and the second one is for words and definitions. If a cast member does not understand a word, then they can put it up on the wall. I make sure a dictionary is present and anyone who is not performing in the scene that we are working on is encouraged to look up the word and write its definition on the paper. Again, I usually put up the first word, partly to show that I am human too and do not know everything, but mainly to establish the fact that it is perfectly fine not to know the meaning of a word and that this is a place of collective exploration and discovery. I would make the action-ing process active – so up on feet rather than sitting around. I would get the actors to find a space on stage – anywhere – and action each line physically by finding a gesture or pose to suggest that action. Many young people have better physical memories than verbal ones, so physicalising the action will embed its meaning deeply and properly ensure their understanding of their character and, ultimately, the play.

Unit-ing and action-ing the play are the first steps to getting the text on its feet – and for some directors they provide the first steps from sitting to standing.

## Blocking

In theatre, deciding where the actors need to stand on stage, and ultimately a physical form for the words on the page, is called blocking. Blocking is partly dictated by the show's design – you cannot enter or exit through a wall for example; but, within the confines of the set, there is a great deal of freedom for the actors to make choices about where they stand and move. The most important thing about blocking, is ensuring that the actors are arranged on stage in a way that helps the audience to focus appropriately and see the play unfold. Some directors tell their actors what to do – where to enter/exit, where to stand, when to sit, move, jump etc. – what Lyndsey referred to as "point and shoot" directors; whereas others allow their actors to dictate the blocking, but might interject with suggestions if a choice looks or feels wrong. Indeed, all of the directors interviewed adopt a free, rather than "point and shoot" approach to blocking, but it is worth remembering that they are working with professional, compliant actors, and so an entirely free approach with a young cast, albeit desirable, is not always possible. However a director chooses to go about blocking, the process of moving from sitting around a table or in a circle, in the early rehearsals, into a fairly open and exposed space, can be daunting – even for a professional actor. So many directors have specific tactics to make that move gradually and to develop physical relationships naturally and spontaneously. Matthew Dunster softens the transition by not sitting around a table in the first place, removing one of the early physical barriers from the outset. His actors have nowhere to hide and are making eye contact from the beginning. The move into the circle is consequently far less daunting. Lyndsey Turner has also used Jeremy Whelan's tape technique in rehearsals to ease the transition between table work and getting the scene on its feet:

> The actors record a scene into a microphone, speaking it in a fairly flat and uninflected way. The scene is then played

back through a set of speakers and the actors involved in that scene then participate in a movement exercise whilst listening to the tape. They can use only three movements – forwards, backwards and standing still. If they feel they are doing something to another person they move towards that person, if they feel that their energy is moving away then they move backwards and if they feel compelled to stay put then they stay put. They do not say anything while this exercise is going on – they are just experiencing the play through their ears and letting their feet do the work and make choices for them. (Turner, 2012)

The director will watch the actors and use the exercise to inspire the blocking of the scene and help to create its architecture. This exercise enables the actors to properly listen to the lines and consider meaning and intention, but it also gets the play on its feet really early, enabling the actors to think about how they inhabit the space. Lyndsey's exercise would be equally valuable for a young cast as it forces them into the space early, and encourages them to listen to the lines and hear their meaning, rather than just reading them and not necessarily understanding their meaning. It creates an open and accessible way of discussing the blocking choices. The director might ask them why they moved and what their physical motivation was. After all, they must have a reason, and that reason will help to tell the story. Does it express the appropriate relationships between characters? They might then mark up the floor with tape to represent the stage and add furniture and just see how the actors behave in the environment. Sometimes the director will need to make the blocking decisions as an individual actor does not always see the bigger picture. As Michael Attenborough says:

A wonderfully camp old actor that I used to work with said, "Darling I do not understand why directors say, 'Come on and stand where you want to.' Surely we all want to stand centre stage don't we? We all want to stand on each others' toes." It paints a wonderful idea of this group of people huddled in the centre of the stage; and there is a little grain of truth in that somewhere. (Attenborough, 2012)

However, most actors would not respond positively to being told to stand in a certain place, and so moving them around the stage requires diplomacy and skill. For example, it would be quite dull to watch a scene between two actors where both choose to sit for the duration of the scene, even if it is a naturalistic piece, so the director must find a way to suggest movement indirectly, asking questions about choices – why did you stay seated for the whole scene? Is there a moment, or shift in attitude, that might make you want to stand or walk away? Equally, in that same scene, the director might need to ask the actors to play unnaturally out front to engage the audience – it is very dull to look at two profiles, so are there any lines where looking out might feel more natural? For young actors, they may well be used to being told where to stand, and so encouraging freedom of movement might be tricky. Exercises that get them moving around the room and saying their lines, or ones like Lyndsey uses where they respond to recordings, are a good starting point.

It stands to reason that if professional actors can feel awkward about getting up on their feet, then so too can young casts. Indeed, young people are often self-conscious and feel awkward about practical work. Some are more confident than others, but even the confident ones can feel uneasy if you are taking them out of their comfort zones. However, your young cast is already at an advantage compared to the professional one as it is likely that you will have done a great deal of practical exploration around the play before you even get to the blocking. If your cast includes drama students, they will already be used to practical work, especially improvising and playing games. Having said that, it is important to remember that they are not trained actors, and they may also have the added complication of being teenagers who are coming to terms with their bodies, and so much like the approach with the professional actor, you need to carefully consider how to get the work on its feet. Improvising and playing games is not the same as saying the lines from a text and making those lines seem believable to an audience, so a whole new set of fears might emerge. Physicalising the actions is a good way to segway into the process of looking at each unit in detail and on its feet. I have also used a similar exercise to the recording exercise before, called Line of Tension, where you ask the characters to move on a line depending on their status in the scene – they can move at any time and they move forward if they gain status, backwards if they lose it, or remain still if the status does not change. Placing a few restrictions on the exercise is usually more useful with young casts as total freedom can be daunting – where do you start? It is sensible for you to have an idea about who should be where and why, but it can be really interesting to see where the actors' impulses lead them to begin with – it may just lead to something unexpected. The additional dimension to this exercise is that I would mark the entrances and exits, so that the actors know where they come on from and where they go off, even though, for now, they are coming to a line. One thing I would definitely do early on is mark up the space. Professional directors do not always do this straight away as they do not want to restrict the actors, but with a young cast it is imperative that they get a sense of the "real" space as early as possible, and I would bring furniture and props and rehearsal doors into that space at the earliest convenience too – again to compliment the fact that young people often have good physical memories. The earlier you can replicate theatre conditions the more quickly and permanently you embed the idea of what it is going to be like on the night. Since most young people will no doubt have experienced "point and shoot" directing, they will not be averse to being told where to stand and what to do. I always like to turn this on its head by doing an exercise that uses images to help with blocking. So, for example, if I wanted to create a busy London street scene, I would search for images on the internet relating to this, and/or ask the cast to source them, and then ask them to recreate those images. This encourages them to create shapes or compositions with their bodies that can be used later. So, rather than needing to place young people in various locations on the stage in order to make it feel like a busy London street, you can use the image as a starting point for brining the scene to life and creating a beautiful stage picture.

Below are my top ten tips for blocking with young casts:

1. What should an actor do with their hands? As little as possible. This might seem like silly advice, but it is meant to help those who do not know what to do with their hands.

As they get more comfortable on stage, they might find that they want to move them more, but it is far better to start with restricted movement and build on it, than to have someone looking really uncomfortable and out of character because all that they can think about is what they should do with their hands.

2. The character's objectives should motivate the moves. Do not move for the sake of moving. I would go as far as to discourage actors from moving until the action requires a move. Conscious moves are better than self-conscious moves!

3. The moves should help tell the story and should not distract from the focus of attention.

4. The positioning of the actors should guide the audience's focus. A simple trick for focusing the audience's attention involves using the other actors to focus the attention for you by asking them to also look at what you want the audience to look at.

5. Be mindful of sightlines – can the actors be seen? The blocking should work for the whole audience, no matter where they are sitting, and should enable them to see everything that they need to see. It is a good idea for the director to refrain from sitting in the same central spot in rehearsals so that you can see the play from a variety of audience perspectives.

6. Sometimes you just need to make a visually interesting stage picture – avoid lines and semi-circles, avoid actors crossing downstage of the action, and avoid having actors standing too close to one another.

7. Avoid too much back acting – the most interesting thing for the audience is the actor's face. Although back acting can be powerful if used consciously but sparingly, and backs and profiles can help focus the action (see point 4).

8. Beware of upstaging. This can be common with young casts, particularly with crowd scenes. Ask the 'extras' to freeze or give them a maximum of three simple, small movements or gestures to use.

9. You must decide how to use stage directions – which ones are useful to you and which ones will you ignore? It is up to you, but do not feel bound by them.

10. When working with crowds on stage, remember that they are a mass of individuals, so start with the individuals. Why are they there? Where did they come from? Where are they going? Actors only make interesting and striking shapes with their bodies when they are acting well and feel secure, so give them that security by exploring all of the characters in the scene, regardless of whether they have any lines or not. See Chapter 9 on devising for pointers on character creation and development.

Once you have unit-ed, actioned and blocked the play, you have taken a significant leap towards bringing the play to life – and you are half way through stage three of the rehearsal schedule. Make sure you work through the play chronologically. As Matthew says:

> If I can get a real sense that the first three pages are tight, then I feel more confident about pages four, five and six. And then I like to look at pages one to six. Then add another four or five pages; and then look at pages one to 14. (Dunster, 2012)

Even if a play plays with time, Michael would still rehearse it chronologically in terms of time because the actors need to understand how it works in real time in order to fully understand the episodic structure. He believes chronology is really important, and is not happy when an actor needs time off rehearsals because he has to work around that, which almost certainly means working out of chronology, and this affects the momentum of rehearsals and the journey of discovery. This is also true when working with young casts – it is better to work through the piece in chronological order, but also make sure they know it in playing order, so that they have both a good grasp of what happens to their character over time, and also good knowledge of the structure of the play. Working with young casts means that it is inevitable that people will miss rehearsals, for a whole host of reasons. When contracting at the beginning of the rehearsal process, it is crucial that you discuss the implications this has on the rehearsal period, both in terms of getting the piece on in a short time-frame, but also on the morale of other cast members – commitment and attendance at all rehearsals is paramount. However, sometimes it is beyond the control of the young person, and so you will need to have back-up plans for how to manage rehearsals when a cast member is missing, particularly if they have a big role. Can someone stand in? Can you rehearse a different scene? There is no magical formula, but it does highlight the need to be extra prepared and to have not just one but multiple rehearsal options up your sleeve.

The play is on its feet now, albeit in skeletal form, so all that is left is to turn it into something that you are happy to put in front of an audience, and this means more than just standing up, inhabiting the space and saying the lines. You now need to consider how your actors will tell the story in the most believable way to an audience – how will they deliver their lines? How will they inhabit the space? What are some of the things that you can do to help tell the story?

## Off-text work

As part of the process of getting the play on its feet with a young cast, you will need to consider whether doing off-text work will help aid their understanding of the play and, in turn, improve the performance of it. By off-text work, I mean exactly what it states – exercises that do not use the text itself, or the words of the play, but do rely on understanding the play and its characters to explore some of its themes and ideas in greater detail. The popularity of off-text work with professional directors varies, with some finding it crucial to their practise, and others avoiding it like the plague.

For Indhu, off-text work helps her actors to understand a scene. They can momentarily forget the text and improvise what this scene is about so that they understand it and the world outside of it. It also helps spontaneity:

> I love setting up improvisations where I will tell one actor one thing and the other actor will not know what to expect. You get something very spontaneous and in the moment which you do not get when working on text because both actors know exactly what is going to happen. (Rubasingham, 2012)

Equally, for Indhu, it helps to explore parts of the text that an actor might find tricky to perform, so if she feels that a reaction is not quite genuine or is forced she will try to find equivalent situations that could help the actor find that moment; that element of surprise or shock. Matthew Dunster also believes vehemently in the value of off-text work, although, in contrast, he does not do it to help the actors, but rather to help himself:

> The off-text work is about going, "right, we are doing a scene in MacDonald's, and we want it to feel like a chaotic Saturday afternoon in a city centre." I get the actors to create worlds for me. (Dunster, 2012)

Matthew uses improvisation to aid the scene. He does not do it to aid character development: "I do not do what happened yesterday or when you first met" (Dunster, 2012), but he might use it to contextualise a scene, for example if a scene starts in the middle of a conversation, he might figure out through improvisation what the earlier conversation was. Lyndsey also uses improvisation to help contextualise the text, for example if there is a really important incident that is mentioned in the play, but is not written into it, she might work through that incident using improvisation.

Richard will also use improvisation, but sparingly, and only if it is helpful rather than an indulgence. He can be wary of it though:

> Some actors are brilliant at improvisation, but it does not necessarily make them brilliant actors. It just means they have got a kind of imagination that works very, very swiftly, and they are quite often actors who are very good mimics. (Eyre, 2013)

For Richard, it is rare that an improvisation solves a scene because you always have to return to the text, and the scene only exists in the text that you have and you cannot paraphrase it. However, it might shed light on something or be useful for an actor. Mike rarely uses it in his rehearsal room. Like Matthew, he might ask the actors to improvise a few lines prior to a scene that opens mid-conversation, but he says that, on the whole, actors resist it too. And, like Matthew, he would definitely not use it to help his actors find their characters:

> The king of improvisation, Mike Leigh, said something very pertinent about this. He said that the problem with starting quite early on with improvisation on a text that already exists is that it presupposes you know who you are. The fact is you do not know who you are; you are finding who you are and so your improvisation can be very distorting and very misleading. It is interesting that he advocates against it. (Attenborough, 2012)

For Mike, off-text work mainly takes the form of utilising expert opinion to aid the actors' understanding of key themes or issues in the play. When he directed *The Knot of the Heart*, a play that tackles the issue of substance misuse, he asked a physiologist who runs a drugs unit at Chelsea and Westminster hospital to come and talk to the cast. He also asked a representative from City Roads, a crisis intervention centre, to talk to the actors.

Doing off-text work with young people can certainly be useful, although I would always ensure that it serves the play and genuinely helps with understanding and character development rather than doing it for the sake of doing it. Also, when working with younger people, it is important to consider the connotation associated with improvisation: the generation of mildly funny material. This is not the most helpful way of thinking about improvisation for a working rehearsal room, and so I would avoid using the word. Instead, I would set up the scenario as it arises. If we take Lyndsey's important incident, for example, where a piece of absolutely devastating news has been delivered off stage, I would ask the cast to comb through the text for all of the facts about it. Taking those facts into consideration, I would then ask them to devise a scene that portrayed the telling of that news as accurately as possible and in keeping with the style of the play. I might even get them to tell it in a different way – gossiping because they overheard it, drawing it as a cartoon, reporting it on the news or as a newspaper article, for example.

Mike's off-text work is also useful, however rather than have someone come in and talk, I might ask them to deliver a Q&A,

so that the cast feel involved and do not switch off. I might even see if there are any short films on the issue, or take them to see someone in an external environment, rather than in the rehearsal room, so that they see that person in their world. The aim of any off-text work should really be to aid understanding and to help the cast realise the play as truthfully as possible, and sometimes that simply means showing them the world of the play. As Lyndsey says:

If somebody is describing an epiphany which they experienced on a trip to the seaside, I would rather not see them waving their arms around trying to describe the coast line, I would much rather they simply held a picture of it in their head. (Turner, 2012)

Contextualising and aiding understanding, through improvisation and utilising experts, may well be enough for the professionals, but with young casts there are other reasons for needing to do off-text work in order to help the play, for example finding the appropriate energy for a scene, playing complex emotions, understanding subtext, being intuitive to the scene, understanding the importance of staying in role and not corpsing, spatial awareness, exploring status, and playing character. Below are a few examples of off-text exercises that might be useful enhancers of the text work:

*Machines* This is the same exercise as the one in Chapter 4, but you would be using it here for a different reason. In Chapter 4 it was thematic – enhancing the creation of the world of the play – but here it is about energy. If the energy in a scene is not right, then this exercise will help to gain a collective sense of what the right energy should feel like. Ask the group to enter the space, one at a time, and make a sound and movement that can be repeated over and over again. The sound and movement should portray their personal sense of the energy you are looking for. Tell the group that this is a collective exercise, so as each person enters, they should think about how their sound and movement compliments or enhances the existing sounds. How does it connect, either physically or vocally, or both? Remember – it is a machine, and machines rely on all of their parts working simultaneously. When you have let the full machine run for a minute or two, tell the group that if you pat them on the shoulder, they need to stand out and observe the machine. The machine should continue even if people are standing out. Pull out one or two people at a time. Ask them if they feel that it reflects the energy of the scene. If not, why not? What needs to change? Allow them to direct changes – to the whole group or to individuals. Put them back in and repeat with new people standing out. Bring the machine to a close and then discuss it. Did they achieve the desired energy? If so how? And how can this be translated into the scene. Invite individuals to talk about how they might play it differently in order to capture this energy.

*Elements* This is another useful exercise to consider generating specific energy. It is also good for thinking about character from a physical perspective. Ask your cast to find a space in the room. Take each of the elements in turn – earth, air, fire and water – and ask the group to find adjectives to describe these elements. For example, air might be light, floaty, buoyant, fresh, fluid etc. Now ask them to move around the space as if they are this element. How would air move? Now tell them that you are going to add a scale to these moves, one being the lowest, most gentle representation of the element, and ten being the highest, most intense representation. If you want to really push them, tell them that their ten is reading as a five, and so they need to up their game – they usually do! To finish, bring them from ten down to one, telling them that one is the human form of that element – so they need to portray characteristics of the element rather than the element itself.

*Transformations* This is a great exercise that can be used to consider the complex emotional journeys that a character might go on in a play. It can also be adapted to consider character development or to consider the views of other characters. I usually do it first using the *All the World's a Stage* speech from Shakespeare's *As You Like It*, just so that they get the idea. Ask the students to create seven frozen images to represent each of the seven ages (or however many images it takes to portray a character's changing emotions in a scene or play, for example).

Now ask them to move, in slow motion, from image to image, on the count of ten. Stress that it must take them exactly ten seconds to move between images – not five, or two or seven, but all ten. Make sure you hold each image for a few beats before you start counting again. Repeat the exercise using five counts, and then just a clap. You could even try switching the order. When you have finished, discuss the characters' journeys. How did their physicality change from image to image, emotion to emotion? Was it easier on the count of ten, or in a single clap? How does it relate to the play? Does their character change emotions much? If so, how quickly?

***Playing the subtext*** This is best done in scenes between two people, although it can work with more. For every actor on stage, you need another actor. So, if there are three people in the scene, then you need six people in total. Ask the three actors to read the scene as normal, but allowing space after each line. The 'other' actors need to stand behind one of the main actors, and after each line they should say what the character really means with that line, or what they might really be thinking or feeling. If the line has no sub-text, then they do not say anything. You can ask the actors to do this on the spot – and it often highlights some interesting and useful interpretations, or you can give them time to prepare it. The first approach makes it quite tough for the "other" actors as it can be difficult to respond in the moment, however it often gives a more spontaneous and honest response; and the second approach obviously enables the 'other' actor some space to think – and allows the actors to feed into the process. It depends on what you want to achieve, but, either way, it usually generates some interesting and lengthy discussions about the characters.

***Stop/Go, and create me a...*** This exercise is really good if you want to encourage the group to be a little more intuitive and/or you want them to react quickly and consider how they might support one another effectively (erring on the side of group dynamics). Ask the group to move around the space in a neutral way. They must ensure that they are balancing the space, not bumping into each other and not talking. If there is a gap, highlight that gap. You want them to start thinking collectively – how do they support each other to keep the space balanced. Now you want them to start to be intuitive. Can they stop together as a group? And then start again. Or touch the wall at the same time? What happens if one person takes the lead? Will they all follow? If so, can someone else take over? How do they, as a group, work as one? This can be really useful to get them moving together and supporting, rather than countering, any moves. I have never encountered a scenario where the group do not want to achieve this unity. Now start to give the group further instructions – as a group, create a washing machine in ten seconds, for example. How do they support each other to achieve this? This can generate some really interesting images, but most importantly it gets the group working together spontaneously.

*Ha!* Much like the above exercise, this is about intuition. Everybody stands in a circle. Ask them to either close their eyes or focus on a point in the centre of the circle. Explain to them that at some point, when you feel that there is total concentration and focus, you will jump forward and shout "ha!" You would like the group to do this at exactly the same time. This usually takes a few attempts, but it is possible. And there is usually some excitement and chatter after the first few attempts, but equally this decreases as they become more confident with the exercise, and committed to achieving a unified "ha!" You might like to nominate other members of the group to lead the "ha!" It is a good idea, in order to up the challenge, to do this anonymously. Ask the group to close their eyes and tell them that you will walk around the circle and that you will touch somebody on the back – that person will lead the "ha!" As the group gets more competent, you could try altering the volume or tone of the "ha!" Can they use their intuition to pick up on this? After playing the game a few times, ask the group when it worked best. How did they use their intuition? How might this help them in the scene or play?

*Trust exercises* One of the biggest challenges with young casts is their ability to stay in role when they are not the central focal point. If you are working on an ensemble piece, this is not usually as much of a problem, but when you are not, it is difficult to get the cast to understand that any fidgeting, and unnecessary scratching of the bottom, detracts attention from where it should be. I would try to get this idea across using some simple trust exercises. My favourite is Falling Circle. In groups of seven, have one person stand in the middle while the other six form a tight circle around them with their hands out in a catching position. The person in the middle should root their feet to the ground, close their eyes, and then fall forwards or backwards. The people in the circle should gently receive the fall, taking a step back if necessary and then just as gently push them back to the centre. The person in the middle should then fall again. Encourage a fluidity of motion, so the person in the middle should respond to the direction in which the people on the outside push them. It should feel like a continuous movement rather than lots of smaller moves. Draw the exercise to a close and ask the person in the middle how they felt. Ask the people on the outside what it was like to guide and support too. Now ask the person in the middle how they would feel if you took away two of the people from the circle, leaving gaps where they stood? You can translate this feeling of uncertainty and lack of support and teamwork back to the performance. Everyone has a role, even if it is one of support. A word of caution – be wary of using trust exercises with a group that has not bonded well, or there are poor group dynamics, as there needs to be a basic level of trust in the group for this to work and be safe.

*Bubble of space* This is an exercise that will help your cast consider the use of space. Start by asking the group to stand in the centre of the room, huddled closely together. Tell them that you will shortly walk through the middle of them, but they need to imagine that you have a bubble around you, with thick walls, that extends to the end of your arms and completely circles your body. They are a little bit like the liquid in a lava lamp – easy to disperse, but they always come back together. When you walk through them, they need to disperse accordingly, allowing you, with the bubble walls, to move through them, before coming back together. I would repeat this using varying sizes of bubbles – an inch wide, the width of the room, two arms lengths etc. The exercise gets the cast thinking about space. You could discuss performance scenarios where you might use this. A small bubble if someone passes wind in a lift. One the size of a room if someone is wildly thrashing a gun around. You can then use this as a point of reference or shared vocabulary in the play – what size bubble of space would your character have in this scene? When she enters, how big is her bubble? Etc

*The power of space* This is a simple exercise that encourages discussion about space and status. Ask a volunteer to enter the space, remaining neutral, and direct him/her to various spots in the space. This works even better if you can do it in the space that you will be performing in. At each point, discuss with the group what the positioning of the actor tells them about his/her status. What if you put them on a chair? What happens if you add more actors? Now secretly give the actor a number between one and ten, one being the lowest status, ten being the highest. Ask the actor to repeat the exercise, but this time, instead of remaining neutral, try to play the status. Does that have an impact on how the audience views the character? What if you add another actor with the same status? Or with a different status?

*We're goin' prowlin' (walk, talk like a T-Bird)* This exercise is a physical one that enables the cast to think about how their character moves. Students often feel more comfortable with the physiological than the physical; they know their character and respond well when being hot-seated, or can write a monologue from that character's perspective etc, but they tend to struggle with physicalising their character – and often walk, talk and move like themselves. Start by asking the group to think of three adjectives to describe their character, for example practical, fun-loving and paranoid. If possible, find a costume – beg, steal, borrow or make it! Ask the actors to move around the space in a neutral fashion, giving nothing away. Now you will lead them through an exploration of how their character could move, starting with their feet and moving up their body to their head. Ask them to consider the following:

- Which way do your feet face? In, out, straight?
- What is the distance between your feet?
- How big or small is your stride?
- Which part of the body do you lead with? Head? Chin? Shoulders? Chest? Tummy? Hips? Knees? Feet?
- Are you being pushed or pulled?

- Are you light or heavy?
- Do you look up, down, straight on?

Have your students explore different options, and eventually decide on a particular way that their character moves. Tell them to be bold and definite with their choices. Now exaggerate them. Now tone them down. Watch and discuss. How does the physicality of a character inform an audience about their emotional state, occupation, status etc? Do they need to adapt slightly?

I would always precede any of the exercises above with the reason behind why we were doing it. For example, if a scene lacked excitement, I would stop it and tell the group that it lacks excitement, and so we are going to try an exercise that will help us create that excitement. These exercises provide creative routes into the text, helping the young actors to bring them to life, and will ultimately help them to perform better.

So now that you have unit-ed the play, actioned it, blocked the individual units, and fully understood its language and story through off-text work, what is next? It is a process of building and refining, and building and refining, until you are ready to put the whole play together. Lyndsey would concur:

> In a four-week rehearsal process you might get three good goes at each scene if you are lucky. The first might be to do with just scratching itches and following impulses. The second might be a little bit more detailed, and then the third might be the version of the scene that is most likely to travel into the theatre with you. (Turner, 2012)

But deciding when to put scenes together and run the whole play is tricky. You do not want the cast to lose confidence if it is a mess, but, equally, the sooner they do it, the more confident they will be in the play as a whole. Michael Attenborough believes that timing is crucial when embarking on a first run:

> It is like judging what the appropriate length of time is between going back to see a show I have directed and opening night. Go back and see it too early and they think, "All right, just give us a bit of elbow room." Go back and see it too late

they are saying, "Help, we want you." It is the same thing for a run-through. If you do it before people are really ready then you run into trouble. (Attenborough, 2012)

If Michael felt it was counterproductive to do a full run-through, he might instead do a run of a character's journey, rather than a conventional run. For example, when he directed *When the Rain Stops Falling* by Andrew Bovell, he ran all of the scenes between the young Englishman and the Australian girl together so that the actors playing those roles got a sense of what their journey was. This could also be a useful transition between running whole scenes and running the whole play for young casts.

For most professional directors, runs come quite late in the rehearsal period, and they can often be quite soul destroying. For Richard, the run through can be monumentally depressing:

You might have been excited by scenes individually, but when you put them together the whole is much less than the sum of the parts. And you need terrific will power and endurance to not get depressed at that point and not communicate your depression to the actors. At that moment it is so important that the director is constructive and has a clear strategy of how it will be pulled together, and what has to be done; and that requires a lot of thinking and planning. (Eyre, 2013)

Equally, the first run with a young cast can be clunky, and it is difficult to gauge when it should happen. I would suggest doing a run, or as Indhu would rather call it a stagger-through or a stumble-through, as early as possible with a young cast. As Lyndsey says:

There is something about the British education system that privileges the scene over the play. There are a lot of drama courses that focus on scene studies or monologues. We have to be careful that we are not producing a generation of people who are trained to run 200 meters, but go to pieces over a longer distance; so the sooner you run things together the better. (Turner, 2012)

Young people will require guidance around the bigger picture, and will need the safety net of knowing the whole play – what comes before a scene and what comes after it. Equally, the British education system, like many others, has fostered a culture of objective setting. All lessons have a set of objectives and these are measured against at the end of the lesson with the students. They expect to know what they are doing and why they are doing it – and they do not have the life experience, or the training, to just trust you. So Indhu's stagger or stumble is better than no run at all.

# 7
# Stage 4: Edit, Bring It Together and Polish

Once the play is on its feet it is time to perfect it. Like Indhu says, it is about adding more colour to a black and white sketch. This can partly be achieved through some of the off-text work in stage three, but there are also many other things to consider in rehearsals to help bring the play together and polish it. This chapter focuses on those other things. Some of them fit neatly into stage four and others run through all of the stages in the rehearsal period. They include: noting the actors, the use of games in rehearsals, what to do when a rehearsal is not going to plan, fostering a good group dynamic and managing behaviour, how to learn lines, the use of specialists to help realise the play, and the role of the stage manager.

## Noting

When you get into running the play, there is a gear change in the relationship between the director and the actors. You are no longer stopping and starting and finding solutions together, but rather feeding back to the cast at the end of the run. In theatre, this is called noting the actors. Different directors note their actors in different ways. For Lyndsey, it is about having a shared vocabulary about the play:

> Because we have worked hard on creating the world of the play, we can reference that a lot. So for instance if you have decided that two friends have a relationship which goes back

20 years, you can then ask the actors whether they might be able to play the scene with a clearer sense of that relationship. (Turner, 2012)

For Michael Attenborough, it is important to know when it is the right time to give a note.

> I never fail to take a note, but there is always a split second when I look at the note and I think, "do I want to give that note now or do I want to give it in a week?" You do not want to stop the actor doing something that was wrong; you want them to find out themselves that it was wrong. In the early stages of being a director I thought my job was to give notes, I over noted I think. I give less now and trust the actor to find it themselves. (Attenborough, 2012)

When to say something is every bit as important as what to say and how you say it. With young people, praise is a powerful thing – it is all too easy to note the things that are not right and forget about what is working well, so make a point of sharing the positives as well as the negatives when you give a note. And make sure any negative note is given constructively – what might they do differently next time to improve? Better still, have them work this out for themselves.

The way that you note young people really does have to be carefully considered. It would be counterproductive to shout at your actors and/or give line readings, with you telling the actor how to read the lines in a way that you like, then asking that this reading be mimicked by them (although this might be a useful tool occasionally if they need help with the line and they really cannot get it, but only as a last resort). I also think that asking an actor to be louder or quieter or angrier is a useless note. If you ask an actor to do a scene more quickly, the first couple of minutes of the scene will be quick but then they will just forget and slow down. But if you give them a reason to be quick, for example, your character's mum is coming back from work any minute and you do not want her to hear what you are saying, then they are more likely to speed all of the way through the scene. Notes need to motivate and be helpful rather than directive. By using the clock, you motivate the actors, which is much more effective than saying "speak faster." I do a projection exercise where I have two actors stand facing each other, nose to nose. The first actor says a line, and if the other hears it clearly, they step back. Then the second actor does the same thing. If the other person does not hear them clearly, they must repeat the line again until they can hear them. Only then can they step back. They keep doing this across a large room, so that as they move out they must project more in order to be heard. In my experience, this exercise is great in the moment, but does not always translate to the stage. They project beautifully when prompted, but can revert to a whisper when back in the scene. So, doing this exercise, but giving an intention, for example it is raining and the traffic is noisy, and you really need the bus driver to hear you, tends to yield better results when they are back in the scene, but it is important that the intention relates to the scene. Essentially, notes need to be quick and efficient, as well as encouraging but specific. You also need to make sure they have fully understood you. Any note is worthless if it has not registered properly. When I note young casts, I tend to follow a specific structure every time so that they get used to how to receive it. I also like to include the cast in the note giving as they will often have noticed something for themselves, and this self-recognition is far more powerful than hearing it from me as they take ownership of it. Below are some simple methods of structuring feedback. They are all useful techniques for general feedback, but open the young people up to giving and receiving constructive criticism, and so when you follow with more detailed or specific notes it does not feel like an attack. If a young person has already highlighted a note during the general feedback, I would not repeat it as they already know it:

*Rose and thorn* With this technique, everybody says one thing that they liked about the run (the rose) and one thing they did not like (the thorn). The thorn must be general though and not personal.

*Fill in the blanks* Ask the cast to use the following sentence to structure their feedback, filling in the gaps with whatever they feel is appropriate: "Next time, I will ... again because ....

However, I will not ... again because ... Instead I will ... This will mean that I give a better performance next time." I particularly like this structure because the onus is on personal responsibility rather than criticising others – what will they do as an individual to make the piece better?

***Bin it. Keep it. Save for later*** This exercise encourages the cast to think about things that they would throw away and not do again (bin it). Things that they would definitely keep and do again (keep it) and things that they might save for another time, acknowledging the fact that some choices might be interesting theatrical ideas that could be used in the future but are not right for this particular performance. Put three big pieces of paper on the wall, with each heading written at the top, and ask cast members to write one thing for each heading on a post-it note and stick them on the relevant piece of paper. Share the results.

***Me – a challenge; you – inspirational!*** Like rose and thorn, go around the circle, but this time you must say one thing that was a particular challenge about the run for you; and one thing that you thought the person to your left did really well.

When I get on to detailed notes, I would keep them brief. I would take time to consider my top three general notes, and then give a maximum of one specific note to each cast member. Anymore, and it will be difficult for them to remember it, let alone do anything about it, on top of the general notes. I like to give only three general notes because somebody once told me that you need to say a person's name three times, out loud, in order to remember it (also a useful tip for incorporating into name games) – and so I figured you could apply this theory to remembering notes – if you give only three, then those three will stick. I would also remember to give some motivation to the note. The other thing to remember about noting young casts is that they need time to just enjoy performing, especially if they are only doing one or two performances of the play. It can be quite soul destroying if you note after every performance. At this stage, you do not want to deflate them, and, if you give them some space and freedom, they might just surprise you. On a three performance run, the last time I would note would be after the dress rehearsal. After the first performance, if I felt it needed it, I might gather the cast and ask them to quietly contemplate the performance, maybe even completing the exercises where they 'fill in the blanks' in their heads, but absolutely no more than that.

In theory, the closer you get to opening night, the fewer notes there should be. However, the opposite is quite often true as the director begins to panic and wants to make sure that he or she has solved everything, and so over notes. But remember, just by saying that something needs fixing, it does not necessarily get fixed. You will soon need to let go, which is difficult, but you have done all that you can and it is now time for the actors to take control.

## Games

It is not a good idea to start a rehearsal with a young cast by ploughing straight into the text. Indeed, this can be incredibly counterproductive as they are used to being warmed-up and eased in gently. They may have just come from a very still and quiet maths lesson, a rainy cold playground, a detention, an exam, a difficult day at school or college, or a dentist appointment. And they may have all come from different places. Your first job as a director is to bring them into the rehearsal room, and focus them for that rehearsal, leaving their baggage at the door. As Indhu says, when working on the two-hander *Stones in his Pockets,* by Marie Jones, she found it really hard work and had to find a way to warm-up her actors:

> We would spend an hour in the morning just gossiping and chatting and catching up. That was part of the warm up because there were only three of us in the rehearsal room and it was very intense. On one hand it looked like we were sitting around chatting, but the trust was building up. We were having a laugh and we were familiarising ourselves with each which relaxed us. (Rubasingham, 2012)

With young casts, the equivalent to Indhu's gossiping is to play a game. Games are pretty controversial in professional theatre.

Some directors and actors love them and others hate them. Mike never plays games in his rehearsal room as he does not feel that they help to blend a company; he feels that the play itself is enough to create connections and enable a company to gel. In contrast, Matthew Dunster believes that games are important, and all of the games that he brings into his professional rehearsal room he figured out through working with young people or community groups. Matthew's reason for using games is mainly to counter the cerebral, static nature of early rehearsals:

> I know how much I want the actors to sit down in the early stages and talk to me and each other, and that can be a very physically deadening experience, and the energy of a game really feeds the brain. I am a bit of a warm-up fanatic. If we have a 15-minute break, when we come back we will do a game; after lunch we will do a number of games. If I am really honest, it is probably more for me than for anybody else. As an actor, I was the one who got to run around, and now, unfortunately, I am one of the people sat in the corner of the room, so I need to keep that side of me alive. (Dunster, 2012)

As both an actor and director, Matthew could see the value in games, but this appreciation is not universal. In fact, many actors absolutely hate them, and do not see the point in them. As Richard says, "half the actors think they are a waste of time and embarrassing because they are infantile" (Eyre, 2013). Richard acknowledges that they work brilliantly for some directors, but they do not work for him. His version of playing a game is about making social relationships and considering how you engender those relationships. This is important with young casts too, and will be covered below under group dynamics. Matthew is also a fan of trying to keep the games from the rehearsal room alive in the play on stage:

> What I really love is when there are traces of the game left in the production. It seems to be madness to me, doing all this wonderful work in a room and then abandon it and replace it with something that is never going to be as exciting as what the research was. (Dunster, 2012)

For him, seeing them in the work validates them. Lyndsey only uses games if they have a genuine relationship to the play, either rhythmically or intellectually:

> When I worked on a Restoration comedy, the company and I learnt to play a complicated card game that was about lying to the other players, storing up a set of cards and then swooping in at the end and taking all their money. The game pretty much reflected the plot of the play, but it allowed us to come at the writing from another angle. (Turner, 2012)

For Lyndsey, the purpose of playing is to aid her actors' understanding of the play. Games can do this for young people too, but they also have other functions. I personally start every rehearsal with a young cast with a game as it focuses the group, gives them time and space to leave their baggage at the door, and, essentially, if they study drama in any capacity, they will be used to starting a rehearsal in this way. However, it is worth bearing in mind that for the half of the group that enjoy games, there is also the other half, like those actors that Richard identifies, who find them embarrassing and childish. This can be as true of young casts as it can professional actors, so tread carefully. The key here is to make them succinct and relevant – do not just play a game for the sake of playing a game, and do not spend too long on them to the detriment of the rehearsal. However, when executed well, games encourage team work, coordination, structure, special awareness, concentration and focus, timing, and they help the actors lose their inhibitions, all within a fun and relaxed framework. I think it is always good to remember that in the majority of scenarios where a director is working with a young cast, the young people will have chosen to be there. They might be doing the play as part of a lunchtime drama club, with a youth theatre, or have opted to study drama because it is a subject they enjoy. Furthermore, games enable the young actors to get stuck in and involved and completely forget that they are honing skills. If you are clever about it, games can also segway neatly into work on the text.

There are plenty of books that provide a comprehensive list of drama games, like *101 Drama Games and Activities* and *101*

*More Drama Games and Activities*, by David Farmer; *Drama Games for Those that Like to Say No*, by Chris Johnston; *Drama Games for Devising* and *Drama Games for Classrooms and Workshops*, by Jessica Swale. But rather than regurgitating those games here, I am going to explain my favourite one and why I use it for virtually every play that I direct with young casts. The game is commonly known as Zip/Zap/Boing, and I use it because it provides a framework and some basic rules for inventing an entirely new game that is thematically linked to the play that we are working on and is essentially created by the young people themselves. I would begin by teaching the cast my variation of Zip/Zap/Boing:

1. Ask the group to stand in a circle, and adopt a neutral position – feet hip width a part, hands by their sides.
2. Start by passing a zip all the way around the circle until it comes back to you. The zip is created by clasping your hands together and pointing them to the person next to you. As you pass the zip, say the word and make the action. The zip should have energy, should move fluidly and quickly, and each participant in the game should return to a neutral position after they have passed it on.
3. When it has returned to you, introduce the boing. Use a boing to change the direction of a zip. You make a boing by turning to face the person who has zipped you, putting both hands in the air and waving them (the British Sign Language sign for clapping) and saying "boing." The zip will then go back in the other direction until somebody boings it again. Tell the group that the zip must go all the way round the circle one before anyone uses a boing. This is to build up momentum and get the game going. Practise this a few times.
4. Now it is time to add the zap. If somebody zips you and you do not want to continue to zip and you do not want to boing either, then you have the option to zap. A zap goes across the circle. You send it across using the same action as a zip, hands clasped together, but you must take a step forward and look directly at the person you are sending it to, so that it is clear who the zap is going to. The person receiving the zap has three choices. Firstly they can accept it, and choose to proceed with a zip to their left or right, and play resumes. Secondly, they can

choose to accept it, but decide to send a zap to someone else (anybody apart from the people either side of them, as that would be a zip, or the person who sent it to them). Finally, they can choose to reject it. They do this by crossing their arms in front of their face and saying "reflect." If the person who sent the zap is rejected with a reflect, then they can choose to zap someone else (anybody apart from the people either side of them, as that would be a zip, or the person who rejected them), or they can proceed with a zip to their left or right.

5. These are the only rules to the game, but they are strict rules. A person is out if they do a boing or a zap before the zip has gone all the way round the circle once, if they zap someone next to them or zip across the circle, or if they reflect a zip or boing a zap, if they make a wrong move (e.g. they do not step forward on a zap) or if any of their moves lack energy or there is hesitation. If a person is out, they sit down. The nearest person to you is now considered to be next to you – so you cannot zap them, even if they are three or four people away.

I would spend the first week or two getting to know the rules of the game. Then I would ask the group to replace the zip, zap and boing with moves that are thematically linked to the play. For example, when working with the MGCfutures Company around Martin McDonagh's *The Cripple of Inishmaan*, the group passed the word "peas" around the circle, and mimed passing a can of peas, instead of a zip. They substituted a boing for "no thanks," and a zap was one of Bartley's lines from the play – "do you have any fripplefrapples/yallowmallows/minteos?" and was reflected with the line, "we have only what you see." As the weeks progressed, the group then added additional rules that they invented themselves. For example, if they said "fecker" the peas skipped a person; if they said "shark attack" (inspired by the *Man of Aran*) then everyone had to swap places; and if someone said, "oh the potatoes," one at a time everyone in the circle had to kneel and say, "you eejit," going all the way around the circle until it reached the person who started it again and they resumed with "peas." The exceptional thing about this game is the sense of ownership that the young people get – I am convinced that they would play it for the whole session if you let them. It encourages competition, but in a light-hearted and safe way, but also relaxes and focuses the group, whilst simultaneously being linked to the play.

Whatever game(s) you choose to use, it is important to remember the following pointers when introducing a new game:

- Keep your instructions simple and concise and break them down into bite sized chunks.
- Do not assume that the group has understood the game – allow them the opportunity to ask questions, ask them to reiterate the rules or have a practice round.
- Be strict with the rules.
- Have fun!

You may also like to tell the group that no matter what they think they know about the game, this is your game with your rules – so forget it! After all, most people take pride in reinventing, adapting and adding to existing games, and this will prevent you from being faced with a select few know-it-alls who want to take over! Indeed, there are numerous drama games in circulation, with numerous variations – so you need to decide which ones work for you and which ones do not. And remember, any game is just a starting point for you to use, adapt, reinvent, and even add new rules! But most importantly for me, games are a way of simultaneously warming the group up, and focusing them.

## Rehearsals not going to plan

One of the most difficult things to deal with when working with young casts, is how to rescue a rehearsal when it is not heading in the direction that you intended. Rest assured though, rehearsals do not always run smoothly for professional directors either. In fact, Mike always assumes that most rehearsals will not go to plan. Likewise, Matthew believes that a willingness to fail actually delivers far better results in the end:

> Experience has told me that you have just got to get on with it and knuckle down. Fail, fail, fail, fail, fail, and eventually something happens. (Dunster, 2012)

For Mike, the most difficult thing to manage is dealing with an actor who does not open up about what is in his or her head and keeps stopping:

> It is tricky when an actor, particularly a central actor, stops rehearsals because they do not feel comfortable with the way it is going but cannot quite articulate where they think it might go, or what the problem is, because everybody is standing around, including me, waiting for them to articulate what it is they would like to try. I always feel as though I am taking a kind of can opener to some actors so I can find out what is going on in their heads. (Attenborough, 2012)

And so he will find a way to help them get through it. Indhu would concur. She believes that a big part of the director's responsibility is to make the actors feel safe so that they do their best work, but, "sometimes it is about just knowing where to stop; and not to flog a dead horse" (Rubasingham, 2012). For Lyndsey, it is about being flexible and willing to change the plan. And she also thinks that the judicious calling of tea breaks is a skill to be mastered – it gives you time to contemplate and make decisions about how to move forward. Like Indhu, she believes that knowing when to stop a rehearsal is of paramount importance. She says that, "knowing when a rehearsal is about to eat itself is a really important skill and there is nothing like calling a little five minute break to rebalance the room" (Turner, 2012).

When working with young people, there are a multitude of reasons for why a rehearsal might not be going to plan. There can be moments when things can get tense or people disagree, particularly when it is about an individual wanting his or her idea chosen, even though it might not be the best idea for the piece as a whole, but there can be a sense of personal pride involved if that idea does not get picked. Young people can often take this as rejection, and feel it much more acutely than a professional actor who has the training and maturity to see the bigger picture. It therefore needs to be handled with care. It might even be wise to take Lyndsey's advice at this point and take a tea-break, or set them on an off-text task, to have a good old think about how to handle it. I would always allow the young person to try out his or her ideas, and utilise the whole group to help decide on the best course of action; but this becomes problematic if 25 young people are offering a different idea as there simply is not the time to try them all. In this scenario, I would try out two or three and again use the group to reach a consensus. In order to try and prevent this happening in the first place though, I always talk about not being precious about ideas when I am setting up a contract with the group right at the beginning of rehearsals. I use the phrase, which is quite horrible but I use it because it is memorable, "be prepared to kill your babies." I always explain fully what I mean by this – that sometimes, for the greater good of the play, we have to be prepared to let go of even the most precious ideas. I also put up a large piece of paper on the wall with the heading 'Baby's Memories' and say to the group that if one of their ideas does not get used, but they really believe in it, then it is probable that it will be useful to them in the future on another project or play. Just because we are not using it in this play, it does not mean it is a bad idea, rather not the right idea in this instance, and so I ask them to document it on a post-it-note and stick it up on the wall for future use.

## Group dynamics

Another reason for an unruly rehearsal might be related to poor group dynamics. If a group is not bonding very well, it would be counterproductive to plough straight into the text, or any pre-text work. Instead, it is important to devote some rehearsal time to doing activities that encourage team-work and good group dynamics – basically anything that gets them to work together. You will probably need to do these throughout the rehearsal period to maintain good group dynamics. Below are some exercises that are particularly useful for group dynamics:

*Lines* Ask the group to get into a line according to: shoe size, age, month of birthday, number of siblings, height, alphabetically according to first name. This must be done in absolute silence, so the group must find a way of communicating non-verbally. This is also a good exercise for exploring status.

***Routes*** In a circle, create a series of patterns. Start with passing your name. The leader should start and then pass on to someone else until everyone has passed their name and it comes back to the leader. When setting up the pattern, ask people to sit after they have passed their name, to ensure everyone is included and it comes back to the leader. You have created a name route around the circle. Now stand up and do it again, following the same route, but without sitting down. Now create a route of numbers. Then colours. Then eye contact. And maybe an action. Run the patterns simultaneously, starting with the group leader. You can make this more complicated by throwing a ball around too. This is great to build on – adding a new route in every rehearsal.

***Counting to ten*** Get the group to stand in a circle and focus on a point on the floor. As a group, they need to count to ten, with one person saying a number at a time. If two people say a number at the same time, they will need to start again. No one should direct anyone else as to when to say a number. The idea is to reach ten, focusing as a team and using intuition. If they make ten, aim for 20, 30 etc.

***Ball in the air*** There are only two rules to this game. The first is that you cannot touch the ball more than once in succession. The second is that the ball cannot touch the floor. The idea of the game is to keep the ball in the air for as long as possible. Every time a person hits the ball in the air, the group leader should count. The aim of the game is to get as many hits, as a group, as possible. Each time you play, try to improve on your previous record.

***Wobbly worlds*** In groups, invent a new world. Give the world a name and its people a way of greeting each other and walking. One person should then leave their group and go to the next. Remember – they only know their way of greeting and walking. How are they made to feel welcome in their new world?

*Team-work scene* In groups, ask the group to brainstorm as many ideas as they can about what makes a good team. Pick their top three. Now create a short scene – no more than three minutes in length, entitled, "Team-work is…"

Some of the exercises already explained for off-text work are also great for team dynamics, like Machines and Ha! (see Chapter 4) and my favourite game, Zip/Zap/Boing, is excellent for helping a group bond, and has the added advantage of being easy to manipulate and make thematically linked (see Chapter 7). Samurai, the game that I use for aiding the creation of a contract, is also good for team dynamics and behaviour (see Chapter 5).

## Behaviour management

Believe it or not, bad behaviour can also be an issue in the professional rehearsal room. Indeed, effective people management is vital in dealing with actors. As Indhu says:

> You are in a room with very different types of people, and a process that helps one type of actor might not help another type of actor. So it is about managing this, and understanding how to communicate differently with different types of people. Talking to someone on a very intellectual, cerebral level might not help another type of actor who is very instinctive and works on an emotional level. It is important to manage the needs of different actors in order to get the best results. (Rubasingham, 2012)

Similarly, a cast of young people is made up of lots of different personalities, all with different needs. Severe behavioural issues tend to be uncommon when it is a group that has elected to be there in their spare time, but they may be possible with a difficult school group. If you have spent time getting the group's buy-in and understanding of the play in early rehearsals, and worked on ensuring good group dynamics, then you are unlikely to encounter a problem with behaviour. The thing to think about, above all else, is why the group is misbehaving. That way, you can do something about it. The other thing worth remembering is that behaviour is usually related to scale. As Matthew says:

> A lot of the difficulties about making work with young people are usually about numbers. If you made a three-hander with three 15 year-olds, you could probably achieve extraordinary things and have a very particular process, but usually you have got 25 of them. So it is man-management, time-management, shifts. (Dunster, 2012)

And so it is important for you to ensure that all 25 are occupied, even when they are not performing, so that they do not get bored. You need to think about how you can make the rehearsal engaging and eliminate the boredom, and think about the pace of the rehearsal and ensure that they are all active with meaningful and useful tasks and activities. Some simple tricks here are to make the audience active observers and ask them to adopt the role of director alongside you when watching a scene – they too can offer suggestions and feedback. Can you get them working on another scene, or learning lines, or writing a rehearsal diary or a blog? Maybe they could design a poster or work on a marketing campaign? Keeping them active with meaningful tasks will really help, although it requires rigorous planning by you.

There are a multitude of possible reasons for poor behaviour. Do they lack motivation? If so, can you relate what they are doing to their own world or real life, and how can you make it fun? Do they lack self-discipline? If so, focus on small targets, use praise and make it interesting. Do they have special educational needs? If so, make sure you have appropriate support, and be flexible. Is the environment a factor? Bad weather? Poor diet? An outside incident or event? A shabby room? If so, what will counter this? Are there any exercises that will relax and focus the group? Remember, they may just also be testing boundaries. If you are new to them, they might just be seeing how far they can push you, so show them who is boss! Below are a few pointers to help with behaviour if it is something that you feel particularly nervous about:

• Be definite – know what you want and what will happen if you do not get it.

- Be aware and know what is going on.
- Be calm and work from the head not the heart.
- Be consistent – in rules and in practice.
- Know what you are doing and work in a structured way.
- Be positive, flexible and persistent.
- Be interested and interesting.
- Be clear and specific.
- Be polite and listen to everyone.
- Remember you are not a friend but a leader – this does not mean that you cannot be friendly though!
- Use the support that is available to you, for example the school system, a teacher, a youth worker etc.
- Be practical and pragmatic in your approach.

One of the key ways of ensuring successful behavioural management is by having a versatile and adaptable approach to your rehearsal. If something is not working, then change it. Equally, if something is worth persevering with, but is not being achieved by approaching it one way, try another way. Above all, do not lose faith in yourself, or what you are doing – if the students are challenging and detect that your confidence is waning then you will lose them quickly – and you will find it difficult to get them back on side.

It is difficult to set out a prescribed list of dos and don'ts when it comes to managing behaviour because every group is different. The strategies below are merely suggestions, based on my experience of working with young people over a number of years, but you will need to find your own way of managing a group by taking on board and/or adapting these suggested ways of working, or find your own:

1. Make sure that your rehearsal is well-planned and has a clear structure. Have you planned some back-up games or off-text work? It is often a good idea, for continuity – particularly if you are working with a group over a period of time – to start and end a rehearsal in the same way, i.e. starting with a recapping exercise (it may have been a week since the group last came together – can they remember what you did last week?) and finishing with an evaluation exercise.

2. Create a contract and make your expectations and boundaries clear. See Chapter 5 for more on contracts.

3. If you make a rule, stick to it – no exceptions. And do not make empty threats. If you warn somebody about not doing something and they persist, you should follow through with any consequences that you have threatened, otherwise the group may think that your words are idle and continue to misbehave. Equally, if you give a specific time limit to an exercise, stick to it. The group will soon learn that you mean what you say.

4. Learn the cast members' names in the first rehearsal – it is so much easier to control a challenging group, or give positive praise, if you can name individuals, and it is much more respectful than "you" or "oi." See Chapter 4 for name games.

5. In that first rehearsal, if the group know each other well, but you need to get to know them, make sure that any name games that you decide to play have an added dimension that is interesting for them, otherwise their attention may wander.

6. Make sure that your instructions for exercises are clear and concise and that your language is appropriate for the group. It is a good idea to ask them to reiterate what you have asked them to do to ensure understanding.

7. Speak in a calm manner – and do not try and talk over the top of the group.

8. Find a way of calling the group to attention. For example, by saying "freeze," using call and response, counting down to one etc…

9. If you ask for silence, or you want to explain an exercise and cast members are chatting, or they are not responding to your call to action, then be prepared to wait. The temptation will be to talk over them, especially if it is only a few people chatting, or it is at a low level, but you will be wasting your voice (and will pretty soon lose it) if you do. By waiting you are reinforcing your expectation of them to listen. Waiting for silence is a really powerful tool, though one that takes confidence to achieve.

10. Praise positive behaviour and spotlight examples of excellence – you want to encourage a positive, encouraging and safe environment for all.

11. If you are working in a school setting, respect, utilise and enforce the school rules – they are tried and tested and have been set by the school for a reason. Sometimes it is just not worth going against them. For example, as a director, you may prefer your students sitting on the floor, but they may be used to sitting on chairs. If the group have the maturity to do as you ask, then great – but do not insist on it if there is likely to be disruptive resistance. Make life easy for yourself!

12. Make a decision about how you structure presentations of work and feedback. Will you spotlight? Will you create an audience? Ask the group to remind you about the expectations of an audience's behaviour. Also – find a way of structuring feedback. You could even give the group the vocabulary if they are struggling, e.g. 'I liked/enjoyed because...' or 'you could try...' Under no circumstances accept negative comments and always praise constructive criticism. The participants need to respect each other too.

13. Do not be afraid to stop an activity if it is not working; or change direction if this will help regain focus.

14. Remember that you are the director, and so you are in control. You need to set the ground rules. They may not like these rules, but it is important to stick to them.

15. Remember that respect is a two way thing. Make sure that you take the time to listen to your cast and respect their thoughts and opinions – everyone should be encouraged to make a positive contribution to the rehearsal and be praised when they do so.

16. Give time to evaluate each rehearsal so that everyone has the opportunity to share their thoughts and opinions – this opportunity for reflection can be positive and empowering for even the most difficult students.

Despite this above advice, I would refrain from going in too heavy handed. You need to find the right balance between friendship and teacher. You are, in fact, neither their friend nor their teacher, and so the role of director is a complex one, and you need to work out how to manage it in a way that suits you and fosters a productive rehearsal room.

## Line learning

One of the biggest hurdles that you might face when working with a young cast is line learning. This is rarely a big issue with professional casts, largely because they are being paid, but with young people line learning is often a challenge. The young people can be brilliant in the room and really switched on, but the following week they will have forgotten everything and will still have their scripts in their hand. Many simply do not have the skills of self-study and the discipline to learn lines. I often try to combat this by using techniques to help line learning in the rehearsal room. For example, tell the actors that they can have their scripts, but that they are not allowed to look at it when they read. Instead they must look at their line, commit as much of it to memory as they can manage in the moment, make eye contact with their fellow actor(s) to deliver the line, and only glance down again to get the next bit of the line. And again, they only look up and speak when they have memorised a sentence or two and can say it without looking. They should continuously repeat this process. This can really slow the rehearsal down, but it does help them to start committing some of the words to memory. The exercise does not preclude the necessity to learn lines at home and outside of rehearsals, but it might make the process easier. Remember too that the young people often hold on to the script for security, so make sure you take it off them as soon as you can see that they know their lines.

You could also suggest mnemonic devices for learning lines. For example, to memorise the colours of the rainbow, the phrase "Richard Of York Gave Battle In Vain" is used, where each of the initial letters matches the colours of the rainbow in order (Red, Orange, Yellow, Green, Blue, Indigo, Violet). Rather than a phrase, images or actions could help. Indeed, I would actively encourage students to walk through their movements on stage whilst attempting to learn their lines as their muscle memory will also jog the brain – a kind of kinaesthetic mnemonic device.

## Specialists

The final thing to consider when working with young casts is whether or not you are going to use specialists to help put the production on. It may be that budgetary constraints dictate that you are the sole specialist, but if you do have the luxury of being able to bring specialists in, by that I mean any or all of the following, depending on the needs of the play: voice or dialect coaches, movement specialists, a choreographer or Musical Director, a fight director, and/or a magician, then it is well worth it. Indeed, if you are working on a show that is really technical, or if it needs dance or a fight sequence or acrobatics, then making sure that this gets appropriate care and attention is really important. Also, it does not have to take away from rehearsal time. As Lyndsey says:

> It took me years to work out that you could rehearse two things at the same time. The spilt call really is a director's friend. If you make the right kind of rehearsal schedule you can effectively double your time, which can do wonders for your productivity and momentum. (Turner, 2012)

The other great thing about using specialists is the access that it gives young people to other industry experts. Most young people want to perform, but quite often this is because it is all they know. In fact I would argue that most people working in non-acting roles in theatre today started out wanting to act too – they just grew up and realised they could still work in the industry, but in a way that was more suitable to their skill set. The earlier young people can be introduced to the other roles in theatre, the better. And if bringing specialists on board really is not possible, you can do this in other ways. Maybe you could take the group on a backstage tour of your local theatre, or organise a Q&A with people who work there.

## Stage management

This is actually something you need to consider early on in the rehearsal period – do you have stage management support, or do you need to conduct stage management responsibilities yourself? Stage management is basically the practice of managing and coordinating the production. The responsibilities and duties of a stage manager vary depending on the stage of the production (i.e., rehearsal or performance) and the scale of the production. A good way to think of it is that the stage manager has overall responsibility to ensure that the director's artistic choices are realised in the final performance, and that these are executed smoothly. Stage management may be performed by an individual in small productions, while larger productions typically employ a stage management team consisting of a stage manager, deputy stage manager and one or more assistant stage managers. During rehearsals, the stage manager typically records the blocking and ensures that cast members stay on script, have the required props and follow the blocking. They are responsible for helping with the rehearsal schedule, liaising with actors about when they are needed for rehearsals, and ensuring that rehearsals run on time. They are also responsible for setting up the rehearsal space, marking it up, and buying and/or sourcing props for the show. As the lighting, sound and set change cues are developed, the stage manager records the timing of each as it relates to the script and other aspects of the performance in the prompt book. Indeed, by the end of rehearsals, this will contain all cues, technical notes, blocking and other information pertinent to the show. Once the show opens, the stage manager controls all aspects of the performance by calling the show – he or she calls the cues for all transitions (i.e., calling the actors to prepare them to go on stage, calling the lighting and sound cues for the technicians to ensure they are acted upon at the right time, and calling scene changes for the rest of the stage management team). In a professional theatre, this is done from the prompt desk, where the stage manager, or deputy stage manager, will follow the prompt book and communicate with the cast and crew via a communications intercom headset. In a non-professional setting, if there is a stage manager, this will often be done in the wings.

It is not always possible in youth or school settings to have a professional stage manager, but it is quite tricky for a director to direct the show and assume stage management responsibilities at the same time. For this reason, I would always advocate having one. Maybe you could you ask a student or someone who is interested in theatre but not in a performing capacity to help. It will make the whole rehearsal process so much easier having someone else in the room who is responsible for some of the more logistical elements of the rehearsal, even if it means they are just creating lists or making notes for you to act on later.

Now that you have worked through the play, and run it a few times, you are ready to move into the theatre – not long now until opening night!

# 8
## Stage 5: Run It, Tech It, Dress It

This chapter focuses on what to do once you have worked through the play and polished it. The key thing is to run the play as many times as you can before you go into the technical and dress rehearsals. This chapter focuses on how you manage these. It also explains previews and deals with how to successfully manage opening night.

### The tech

The technical rehearsal, always referred to as "the tech" in professional theatre, is when the technical team and actors come together to work out exactly, in minute detail, how the play is going to work from beginning to end, scene by scene, on the stage with all of the technical elements added to the performance. Of course, prior to the tech rehearsal, the technical team will have got the performance space ready – referred to as a "get in" (literally getting the scenery and props into the space, after – believe it or not – the "get out" of the previous show, if there was one) and "fit up" (getting everything ready to go). The director tends to lead the tech, but is supported by stage management and the technical team. Whether you are moving into a professional venue, a studio with limited sound and lighting equipment, or a school hall or space without technical support, you will need to incorporate some kind of tech. The more technically demanding the piece, the more time you will obviously need. One of the things that I would do before the tech starts, but after the get-in and fit-up have happened, is to take some time for the cast to familiarise themselves with the new space – unless, of course, you have been rehearsing in it all along; although, even then, it is certain that some tweaks will need to be made to it. And if not, you will have the luxury of running it a few more times.

Below are a few tips for managing the tech:

**Organisation and planning is essential.**

Know who is doing what and why, and have a solid plan. In the professional theatre, the production manager will have created a schedule for tech week. If you have someone production managing your play, check the schedule with them, and make sure the young people are fully aware of when they need to be in and until what time. For Indhu, the plan is crucial, even if you deviate from it, as she believes that it provides "a really good base – a foundation to work from" (Rubasingham, 2012).

**Preparation is key to making a tech run smoothly.**

Your work should begin in the rehearsal room, not the theatre. Indeed, use the rehearsal period to introduce any new elements, rather than waiting until the technical rehearsal to do so. As Indhu says:

> When actors get into a tech, it is getting nearer to opening night, and that is when the tension can rise. (Rubasingham, 2012)

It is a good idea to alleviate this tension wherever possible. If there is sound or music, start using it by the end of the rehearsal process, and bring in props and costumes too. What you want to avoid is unnecessary surprises for the actors. These may change slightly when you get into the theatre, but at least they are not new. The last thing that you want to do is unsettle your actors.

**Plotting lights and sound cues in advance is crucial.**

It is imperative that you know what you want to achieve before the tech, so you should meet with your lighting designer, sound designer or technician during rehearsals so that you do not waste time on this during the technical rehearsal. If you have a lighting designer attached to your production, make sure you set aside sufficient time to work with them properly. Lighting is complex. It not only enables the audience to see the actors properly, but it can also focus attention and create mood and atmosphere; but, most of all, it can really elevate your performance if you get it right. Equally, sound is complex. If you have a sound designer to work with, then they will be able to source all of your sound effects. They get them from an array of places – the BBC sound library, the internet, and/or their own or a theatre's archive of recordings. You can source these yourself too. Be wary with sounds though – do they aid the performance, or do they sound clunky and ridiculous? Do not be afraid to lose it if it does not work. My personal preference is the fewer the better, unless I am working with a sound designer who I really trust to make those choices for me. Equally, I would be careful about using music to underscore action. Whilst it can work, and really serve the scene, it can also detract from the action. And remember, this is theatre not film.

**Be calm.**

As Richard says, "It does not help anybody if you get neurotic and start shouting" (Eyre, 2013). This can be a stressful time, but if you remain calm you will achieve so much more.

**Think about time.**

In professional theatre, the tech time can be anything between one and three days, depending on the demands of the production. This sounds like a long time, but in reality it is not. As Matthew says, "I think I am probably at my most controlling and anal during tech time, but that is just because there is so much to do and so little time, and you have just got to push, push, push" (Dunster, 2012). How much time do you have? Use it wisely.

**This is also the time to fix problems.**

Mike likes to use the tech to improve the actors' projection. He wants them to know when they are audible and when they are inaudible:

> When the actors come onto the stage for the first time in a tech, I tell them that I want them to do it at performance pitch. (Attenborough, 2012)

Other problems that were not perceived problems in the rehearsal room may also arise. A sound effect might sound wrong; a door handle may be difficult to use; or a costume change that you thought would work might now need some tweaking. This is the time to find solutions to those problems, as quickly and efficiently as possible.

When working with young casts, one of the biggest things that will invariably need fixing is the use of space. No matter how much preparation you have done, when the cast walk into the space for the first time they can be overwhelmed, and so a large part of the early tech will be devoted to spacing issues. If possible, try to get access to the set and stage before the technical team is called, because you are likely to want to spend some time resetting people and familiarising them with the space. When it is time for the technical team to arrive, follow in the footsteps of the professionals – make sure that you are organised and fully prepared.

In the last rehearsal before the tech, I like to do a number of exercises that re-familiarise the cast with the play, after all, there will be lots of standing around and a need for them to think and move quickly, so you really do need to have a shared vocabulary when it comes to talking about the play to enable the tech to run smoothly. The last thing that you need is a cast member asking, "What bit is that?" So, do they know it as Act Three, Scene Two or do they know it as The Lovers' Quarrel? I would also devote at least 15 minutes of the final rehearsal to talking them through what will happen in the tech, and why it is important. I would stress the need for them to remain focused and alert, and be honest with them by telling them that some of it will be dull – lots of standing around and waiting. It is really important for them to know this in advance in order to manage their expectations; and if they are aware of it, they are less likely to get fidgety or distracted. Indeed, one of the hardest things to manage in a tech is boredom because it leads to things being really unfocused and can be a vicious circle – the more bored the performers become, the more unfocused they get, and the more unfocused they get, the more bored. Lyndsey equates this to, "brains going into the equivalent of standby mode on a laptop" (Turner, 2012). The problem with this is that the minute you ask them to start again at a certain point, they are lost and distracted and so you lose time trying to regain that focus. The key to minimising this is through ensuring that the cast know the play inside out and back to front. Below are a few exercises to use in preparation for the technical rehearsal:

*Italian run-through* This is an exercise where you get the cast to run through the whole play at lightning speed, massively paraphrasing their lines (and usually getting a bit muddled!) It is really great for a little light-hearted fun, but also to imprint the running order firmly in their heads.

*Map of the play* This is an exercise that involves working individually, ideally on the set or in the actual space if possible. Ask them to walk through their own individual characters' journeys in the play, entering and exiting in the appropriate places. They do not need to play any of the scenes, just mark the moments of entry and exit, and where they move if they are on the stage for a while. Again, this exercise helps to imprint a physical memory of the play.

*Book Ended Headlines* This exercise assumes that you have given each unit or scene a headline. Start with the first unit or scene. Say the title of it followed by the word "beginning," then again followed by "middle," and again followed by "end." Ask the actors to move into the appropriate positions for that part of the unit or scene, and freeze until they receive the next headline/position from you. Work through the whole play in the same way, chronologically, allowing the group to make mistakes and find the right spots. I might do this a couple of times to really embed it. Next, mix up the order. Initially this might be chaos, but the more you play, the more they will get it, thus improving their awareness of moments in the play in preparation for the tech.

***Prop and costume run*** This is similar to the **Map of the play**, in that they need to enter and exit appropriately, but it is specifically focusing on ensuring props and costumes are where they should be. If possible, mark up a backstage area in the rehearsal room so that your actors get a sense of the space both on and off stage before they even enter the playing space. This exercise will help them to grasp their physical score, and they will get used to waiting in a fictional backstage area to go on. This is something professional actors just have in their blood stream from years of experience and years of training but it is new to some young performers, so giving them a sense of where they are at any given time can make a tech and dress rehearsal run more smoothly. If I was feeling ambitious at this point, I might do another **Italian run through**, but insisting that everyone was true to their entrances and exits and their **Map of the play**, complete with props and costume. Again, it might be slightly chaotic, but you will be surprised at how much of it sinks in. It would certainly be a slower **Italian run-through**!

***Help!*** The final exercise that I would do with the cast would be one that is designed to help them if they dry on stage. It will not necessarily help them to remember their lines, but it will help them to relax and recover the moment. It is a ten second exercise that will relax them. Have them play something really energetic and fast paced – maybe immediately after the previous exercise as they will probably be feeling pretty frazzled! Ask them to find a space in the room and find a point on their body to focus on – maybe their hand or knee. Tell them to say the word "relax" in their heads. Tell them to physically drop their shoulders, and breathe out. Finally ask them to say, in their heads, "I can do this." Explain that this is the four stage process that they should use if they dry on stage. It might feel like ten minutes, but it will actually only take five seconds and will give them some thinking space. Remind them that they know the play really well now, so would be able to improvise their way out of most situations without an audience realising anything out of the ordinary had happened. But this is a good technique to help them out of a difficult scenario.

Once in the tech, there are a number of tactics that will help you to ensure that it runs smoothly and will minimise the loss of time. I would spend a good 15 minutes at the beginning of the day allowing the technical team to introduce themselves to the cast and tell them what their role is. As Lyndsey says, it is a good idea to, "get everybody to meet everybody else so that you do not end up with a group of performers wandering around like bored animals on the set, whilst another group of people ferociously press buttons in the dark" (Turner, 2012). It is important that the young performers understand exactly what is going on in the dark, and I find that the more young people know, again it goes back to the current education system and objective setting, the happier and more compliant they are.

If you need to stop the tech to get a light right, for example, it would be a good idea to explain this to the cast. Tell them why you are stopping and where you will be picking up from when you start again. I usually also invite them to sit down where they are or give them a specific on-the-spot task. Although this is mildly disconcerting for the technical team, I find that advance warning prevents any grumbles. I often use a projection exercise here. Like Mike, I want them to work through the tech at performance level, but this is difficult when they are continuously stopping and starting as they lose momentum. So, I would ask them to pick a line from the play, and ask a cast member who is not in the scene, or anyone who is free and willing, to stand at the back of the auditorium and lead the exercise. I would make sure that I had lead the exercise a few times myself already, so that the person leading it while I am sorting out the technical issue would already be aware of how to lead it. It is a simple conductor and orchestra style exercise. The leader acts as a conductor and has four possible moves: point to the actor that they want to speak; move their arm up to indicate louder; and move their arm down to indicate quieter (although this one is rarely used!) The final move is a thumbs up – which he or she will give if they are happy that the actor is perfectly audible from the back of the auditorium. The actors can do this no matter where they are on stage, thus not interrupting the flow of the tech if we need to move on quickly.

The final thing that you might want to consider at the end of the tech, although some professional actors leave it until the dress rehearsal, is how you are going to deal with the curtain call. Your young cast have worked hard, and this is their moment to shine, so make sure you take the time to rehearse it. Nothing is worse than a group of actors reaching the end of a play, the audience clapping and cheering wildly, to suddenly realise they do not know how to take their bow. They just look awkward and embarrassed. Make sure you set it, decide who is leading the bow, and make a decision about whether they should come back on or not for a second one.

## Dress rehearsal

Once you have worked your way through the play, and ironed out any problems, you are ready to do a dress rehearsal. In professional theatre there are often two dress rehearsals; the first enables a full run with all of the ironed out technical issues – it is the first time that the stage management team have the opportunity to run the play and so it is also sometimes referred to as a technical run; and the second one is really for the actors, allowing them to embed all of the changes and take ownership of the play again in its new and elevated setting. This is time for you to sit back and watch. I often move around the auditorium, sitting in different seats, just to see how those audience members who are not sitting in the traditional director's position in the centre of the stalls will view it. I try to be as objective as possible, but that is sometimes hard when you are so close to it. Where possible, I invite trusted colleagues, friends and even other young people into the second dress to be objective eyes. And I would take time to get their feedback after the performance. For me, the final dress rehearsal is the equivalent of previews, since I will endeavour to invite a small audience, and may still make changes to the show.

## Previews

In most professional theatre productions there will be a preview period. This is a select number of the early performances, open to the public but usually at a reduced cost, that precede its official opening. The purpose of previews is to allow the director and the rest of the creative team to identify problems and opportunities for improvement that were not found during rehearsals, and to make any necessary adjustments before theatre critics are invited to attend. The duration of the preview period varies from theatre to theatre. It is unlikely that any production with a young cast will have a preview period, as the length of the run is likely to be quite small – a few days rather than weeks. However, the dress can be treated as a preview. I would only call the cast again before the show opens if significant changes were necessary.

## Opening night

In professional theatre, opening night is the first night after the preview period and is the moment when the play is finally ready. It is also usually referred to as press night as it is traditionally the night when the critics are invited to review the show. It is treated with much celebration and usually involves an invited audience rather than a paying one, and often a celebratory post-show party. In contrast, opening night for a young cast is likely to be its very first night in front of an audience, which may well be its only night in front of an audience, since a preview period is unlikely and it is also rare that it will be reviewed in any way. However, the challenges of coping with opening night can be tricky. The play may feel under rehearsed. The young cast may be incredibly nervous or over excited. You will need to deal with these eventualities if and when they arise. Many of the activities already cited in the book will help to focus or bring energy up or down, as will the "help" exercise used to help when an actor dries on stage. If you have followed the five-stage rehearsal process properly, and utilised the exercises to prepare for the tech and dress, then you should not feel under rehearsed. Most of all, try not to worry. The majority of your work here is done, and it is now over to the young cast to share this play with an audience. Enjoy it!

# 9
# Devising Theatre

I have decided to dedicate a chapter to devised theatre because it is a really popular way of working with young people, and a way of working that most of them will have experienced in some capacity in their school setting. Indeed, devising is on the drama curriculum in schools and is taught on drama courses in further and higher education, and often forms the basis of project work for youth theatre groups, so it is clearly a widely accepted form of theatre making. However, I still have drama teachers ask me how to do it – it is clearly not something that is covered fully on training courses for drama teachers – another reason for including a chapter on it. Indeed, devising is a great way of working with young people as it places them at the centre of the theatre making process, often making the connection between the young people and the work much tighter. Because they generate and help to shape the material, they have a greater sense of ownership over it.

But what is devised theatre? It is certainly a broad concept. Put simply, it is a form of theatre where the final performance comes from an idea, or set of ideas, that is explored and developed collaboratively, usually by actors, but also utilising other specialists, rather than originating from a writer or writers. Devised theatre usually culminates in a script, rather than starting with one, directly opposing it with the dominant form of literary theatre tradition. It is different to improvisation because it results in a fixed form; indeed any improvisation is confined to the creation process, and either a writer, director or the performers themselves, will use it to generate material and decide exactly what is to be included in the final piece, and how that fits together, rather than being the final piece itself.

It is difficult to pin down a concise history of devised theatre, and this is not the aim of this chapter as there are a number of books that already deal with this in detail, like *Devising Performance: A Critical History*, by Deirdre Heddon and Jane Milling, and *Devising Theatre: A Practical and Theoretical Handbook*, by Alison Oddey. Frantic Assembly have also written a book on their devising methodology – *The Frantic Assembly Book of Devising Theatre*, by Scott Graham and Steven Hoggett. These books are fantastic resources that clearly illustrate the fact that devising is complex and multifaceted and there is no one prescribed way of doing it, much like directing a scripted play. Indeed, every group of collaborators will have different ways of approaching the creative process. And what method the collaborators will use depends a great deal on the style of the performance group. For example, a group which makes naturalistic theatre may start with building characters and then gradually begin to build narrative strands together out of character-based improvisations. In contrast, a physical theatre group, like Frantic Assembly, might take a theme or an idea and explore that physically, creating shapes and motifs with their bodies as a starting point.

For the purposes of this chapter, and because the rest of the book is focused on text, I am narrowing my definition of devising to devising from text, either using text in any form as a stimulus for creating work or creating performance by adapting an existing story or novel. There are many other ways to devise, but I am most interested in the process of devising with text as stimuli. Indeed, most of my recent work, both at the Almeida and for the Michael Grandage Company, has involved creating devised response pieces to the plays that these companies produce, and I have become really interested in how one text can inform an entirely new one. The final piece that is created may bear no obvious connection to the original work, as the devising process may have taken us on an entirely different journey, but nonetheless it started by reading or watching it.

The directors that I have interviewed thus far are predominantly directors of existing plays. Whilst some have dabbled in devising, it is not the art-form that they are known for. For this reason, I interviewed two additional directors for this chapter – Annabel Arden and Robert Icke. Annabel Arden is co-founder of acclaimed theatre company Complicite. She has adapted a novel for stage – *Lion Boy*, a children's and young adult's fantasy trilogy written by Zizou Corder (the shared pen-name of British novelist Louisa Young and her daughter Isabel Adomakoh Young). Robert Icke co-wrote and co-directed an adaptation of George Orwell's *1984*, with Duncan Macmillan. Both Annabel and Robert have taken novels and adapted them for the stage, devising with their actors and workshopping ideas as part of the process, and so it would seem that when devising the role of director becomes director-writer. They are acting like the writer, in that they have to ask some serious questions about how one form of the text can be translated into an entirely new one that will be well received by an audience. Interestingly, Robert and Duncan also turned the notion of having a separate writer and director on the production completely on its head by both doing both roles:

> Duncan and I both work as writers and as directors – and we realised early on that we did not want to make this show with one of us as writer and one of us as director. Collapsing those two roles meant we shared joint responsibility for both text and production – and this turned out to be a massively freeing and collaborative choice. (Icke, 2014)

It is of course possible to devise without a director, and many companies do, but when working with young people I would always advocate director-led devising for two reasons: to ensure an outside eye for the work – it is quite difficult to judge how something is working if you are in it; and because young people tend to work better when they know who the voice of authority is and they are used to working in a structured way.

So, why choose to create work from an existing story? From my experience this is much easier, regardless of who you are working with, as devising from a theme or issue can be too broad and conceptual. Indeed, the young people find it hard to narrow the theme or idea down and it can feel quite intellectual, which is the opposite of the state we need to be in to devise.

A specific story or piece of prose usually yields far better results. Annabel agrees:

> It is difficult to make self-generated work. I think you have to be very strongly focused in movement to do that, and you need a very high level of technique in the participants. If the technique is not there, you need a very strong starting point, so I would take a story. (Arden, 2014)

Annabel always starts with stories when devising. I like it too, mostly because young people find it easier to engage with narrative, and there is a danger when devising from a theme or idea that it just becomes a series of episodes or unconnected scenes, rather than something with a plot and defined characters, which, in my opinion, is harder for the young people to love and own because it does not always make sense to them. Indeed, the more devising I do, the more I think it has to have substance. In some of my early work, I knew it looked great but it did not always hang together, so now I strive to achieve both something with substance and something that looks great. And substance is certainly served by having an existing story. So, how do you choose that story? This is very difficult. As Annabel says:

> It is what takes the longest time and depends on whether you are working entirely solo, where as the director you are going to make the choice, or if you are working with a group, and then the choice has to mean something within the context of the group. (Arden, 2014)

Annabel's point here is the biggest decision you will need to make. Are you choosing the text or are the group? I would always advocate the former, in the same way that you would choose the play you are going to direct. Indeed, many of the pointers in Chapter 2 about choosing a play would be useful here as you are still embarking on a piece of text that will be performed on stage in some way, albeit altered from the original. The reason that I would choose it myself is twofold: it eliminates the need to factor in how you are going to fairly and collectively make that choice, and ensure that everyone has a connection to it; and because you are already up against it in terms of time. Before you are able to embark upon the five-stage rehearsal process outlined in Chapter 3, you have to make the play, adding a sixth stage to the process. By not starting with a script, you have to devote rehearsal time to generating it, to the sacrifice of refining and polishing. And so the sixth stage actually needs to come before stage one, and you will probably need to give it around 50 per cent of your overall rehearsal period, squashing the remaining five stages into the other 50 per cent thus effectively halving the time spent on taking it from page to stage. Although, it is worth noting here that a lot of the early rehearsal work of stages one and two will be covered through generating the material, and the students will also have been up on their feet from the very beginning, easing the transition from "table work" to blocking. The key thing to remember is to give enough time to stages four and five – it is easy for a devised piece to feel under rehearsed because too much time is spent generating material and too little time spent putting it together and rehearsing it. This is definitely something to be wary of – you really do not want your cast to be running the piece for the first time at the tech.

I would concur with Annabel – it is important that you feel a strong personal connection to the story, for whatever reason, because you have to envisage the work. As Annabel says, "to a certain extent you have to embody the work. You are the work. It has to mean a lot to you. It is not just that you think it is good. You have to connect with it" (Arden, 2014).

For Robert, it was crucial that he was doing something entirely new:

It is important that when you set out you have got some sort of key to the text that you feel nobody else has found before. There has got to be some way in, or something about the approach, which makes you think you are going to be able to create something more rigorous or in some way more interesting than any other previous version. (Icke, 2014)

For both though, and for you, it is about working out what you think the story or novel is doing. What job is it doing in its current form and how can you do that job in a completely different medium? How can you make the same formal demands, and the same demands on an audience, that, for example, Orwell or Zizou Corder make on their readers? Or do you need to?

If you have chosen the text yourself, how do you ensure that your young cast connect with it too? As Robert says, "You really want to make something with the cast that they really feel invested in; that will only make them more creative and therefore make the show better" (Icke, 2014). Because it is director-led and will culminate in a final script, many of the pointers and exercises already cited in this book are equally relevant and transferable to this way of creating theatre – at the very least, they will need to be applied once the final script has been created. By getting to know the text, exploring its plot and characters, and finding a way of presenting these dramatically, the work should organically become the property of the group. As Annabel says:

> You have to make the group as connected as you are with the source material – an intimate connection. It is difficult, and you need to pursue it on rational, intellectual, and very strong emotional grounds. Why do we want to do the story? What is the story about? What does it tell us? Why is it useful for the world? How can we do it well? What is it that excites us about how we might realise it? (Arden, 2014)

All of these questions are useful starting points when exploring the stimulus text. You must enable the young cast to feel free to take the source material and develop it, even if the original idea was not theirs.

Once you have chosen your text, much like choosing a play, you will need to consider what needs to be done before rehearsals begin. With devising, this depends entirely upon how much time you have for rehearsals. If you have a very long time in rehearsal you can risk going in with very little, just the script and a few ideas for exploring that off the page. However, if time is limited and you have to get the show on by a certain date, then you need to be more prepared. For both Annabel and Robert, there was a limited rehearsal period and so both had to have something approaching a rehearsal script before they started, which meant adapting the original text themselves. For Robert, this was a long nine or ten months of discussing it on a daily basis with Duncan, sometimes writing together, sometimes independently:

It was a process of coming to really understand the novel: to really get right under its skin rather than just taking a quick look at its face. It would be really easy to just take the dialogue out of the novel, copy and paste it and then write some stage directions, but of course it would not work as you would only create an imitation, a secondary experience rather than something that feels immediate and built for its new medium. (Icke, 2014)

For Annabel, adapting *Lion Boy* was a particularly tricky task because not only was it three novels, these novels came out of a mother telling bed time stories to her little girl, where the rules were that anything goes:

If the little girl said, "Let's have a whale," then there had to be a whale, so structure was not important. But structure is important in theatre, so when you are trying to make something structured out of something with no structure, the first task is to decide on form. What kind of form are you going in employ? By that I mean are you trying to write a three act play? Are you going to have text or no text? (Arden, 2014)

Very loosely, form means the theatrical style of the piece. Traditionally this is the type of drama that it is – tragedy, comedy, tragicomedy, melodrama, farce, musical etc – any term that helps define the type of theatre being presented. Some recent drama, however, defies definition – its form is ambiguous. Form is complicated because it could be argued that the form of every play is unique because no two plays are exactly alike, but there are certain identifiable characteristics that are common to different plays and it is these characteristics that help to define the form.

For Annabel, one of the charms of *Lion Boy* was its sophisticated prose and so she wanted to do a young person's show where the prose remained sophisticated; where they had to listen to the words:

> We decided on quite a strict story telling form, where nobody would ever quite speak to each other on the stage, they would only speak to the audience. From this, it became clear that the story was really all about Charlie, and so the piece required a central actor and a chorus. Once you have made those choices, it determines everything else. (Arden, 2014)

For Robert and Duncan, after lengthy discussions about the different influences and possible versions for the novel on stage, they decided that they wanted to be authentic to the novel:

> Initially, we thought the novel was good, that it would make really good theatre but that we would need to add a lot to it, change lots and really jazz it up. However, we fell in love with it: we discovered that it is actually a really great novel, really complex, and of course when you discover mind-expanding complexity in something you want to share that complexity no matter how difficult it is. The more we got to know the novel, the more we wanted the theatre version that we were making of it to hold all of the exciting things we found in it. (Icke, 2014)

Both Robert and Annabel could have chosen different paths for adapting the novels, as there are a million other ways that they could have done them to create very different shows, but they had to make a choice in order to move closer towards the final product. Indeed, when devising, making decisions is paramount for moving forward. You cannot tell an entire novel in two hours so you have to select what you will tell and how. And sometimes you might make the wrong choices, but that is fine as you will always have the original text to go back to.

Both Annabel and Robert spent time workshopping their ideas in order to help adapt the original text; and both spent considerable time on the adaptation. *1984* took just shy of a year to prepare for rehearsals and *Lion Boy* took four years, not consistently but about two weeks a year, or a couple of weeklong workshops, and a lot of thinking time. Annabel worked with a small group of people who she had known for a long time and trusted to explore the text in a series of workshops. In the first one she explored the nature of chorus and storytelling. She prepared the first half of the script herself, from almost all of the first book: "I filleted it, highlighted it in yellow, and re-typed it into a useful script that we could use for the week" (Arden, 2014). During that first week she discovered that the story telling worked fine and that the central character had to be extremely charismatic. She also realised that the portrayal of the lions would need resolving, and so in the next workshop she explored masks and puppetry and shadow play to explore how you could represent animals. She came to the conclusion that she did not like any of the ideas and she was determined to do the animals with absolutely nothing:

> So you have to give yourself one task, in a sense, per workshop. It is also important to have the reassurance of a group of people around you, whether its producers or a friend who is a designer or close colleagues who are actors. (Arden, 2014)

After four years and finding a writer, in fact a series of writers, she went into rehearsals with something approaching a rehearsal script which of course then got changed a lot. Equally, Robert workshopped the script before the start of rehearsals:

> One workshop tested out an early draft of the script – a way to hear the whole play early in its growth – and purely aided the writing process. A second, much later, was more practical: exploring how we could use video and the controversial question of how captivating a live video feed was when you couldn't see the actors themselves. (Icke, 2014)

It is up to you whether you want to do any work on adapting the script before rehearsals begin, or testing out ideas through workshops, or whether you will do all of that in the room with your cast. This might largely be determined by the length of your original text. Robert was adapting a long, classic novel and Annabel was adapting three books into one play – so adapting and selecting with the cast, without any pre-rehearsal workshops would have been really tricky. I often do some of the pre-rehearsal workshopping in the first few rehearsals. With a young cast, it is unlikely that I would work with a novel, but rather a poem or a short story, because of time. Like Annabel, I would highlight and fillet the text, but I would do that with my cast – what words jump out at them? What lines? If you had to tell the story using ten of the lines, which ones would you choose and why? This is essentially a dramaturgical exercise – you ask them to make choices about the most poignant parts of the text to see if those choices hinder or work for the overall narrative.

One of the most important things about devising is getting the group dynamics right early on. I would spend a lot of time in the early rehearsals concentrating on the group dynamics exercises from Chapter 7. This is equally true of the creative team. Robert and Duncan had an unwritten rule that they both had to agree on something before it went in to the final piece and, because they knew they were doing it, they always had to find something to go into the gap. Getting the group to work well together and gel is so important with devised work. Annabel goes further:

> To make a group, you have to share a physical vocabulary in order to make the group function. I do this in lots of different ways, partly drawn from the movement work of Moshé Feldenkrais and partly from a huge rag bag of stuff I have collected, but basically making people move together and play together. Play games. Play improvisations. Really learn about the actual nature of each other's being through the body so that you are instinctively linked like a good football team. It is a long process. It's about sensitivity. It's about openness. It's about lightness. It's about being able to pick up signals from each other. It's about being able to enter into an imaginative situation. It is play. It is what children do when left to themselves – they play. (Arden, 2014)

Both Annabel and Robert use games in their rehearsal room, which is at odds with most of the directors who start with a play text. However, Annabel cites caution: "Games only work if you love doing them, and it only works if the games or the play or movement bears a real resemblance to the material that you choose"

(Arden, 2014). Similarly, Robert believes in a shared vocabulary and a sense of play. He believes that table work, sitting around, underlining things, and talking things through, does not really help the actors. This sense of play is evident in one of the exercises he created for the show. He wanted to create an atmosphere that allowed the actors to experience some of the uncertainty of the book:

> We played some tricks on the actors to make them paranoid. We changed slight aspects of their surroundings, very subtly, just so they would be aware that things were changing, so that they would experience what it felt like to not be able to trust yourself. (Icke, 2014)

He would spend considerable time in rehearsals devoted to devising scenes. He spent a whole afternoon exploring dreams. Sometimes it would feed in really specifically, other times not at all, but it would always lead to further exploration:

> The first dream improvisation established that there is only ever one dreamer and we do not conventionally have two dreamers inside the same dream, which sounds obvious but it is was very helpful dramaturgically. So dream improvisation two was to take the dreamer out of the room. The rest of the actors would then devise something that was going to happen to that dreamer when they came back into the room – their dream – and they would be led through it genuinely not knowing what was going to happen next. (Icke, 2014)

Equally, he invented a game he called hive mind. It involved the actors all jostling together in a big pack, like blood cells moving around trying to be one unit, and if anyone separated from the pack the others would point at them and they were out. They would then leave and the rest of the group would continue to work. The aim of the exercise was for the actors to keep themselves in the hive by maintaining contact with the other people:

> I then started to mix that up by privately giving them alliances and saying, "when we do that again I want you to protect this person," or "I want you two to work together."

You would start to see that happen, and in a really small way they experienced some of the paranoia of the book, but it also really taught them to be aware of what the whole group was thinking. (Icke, 2014)

Robert's choice of game simultaneously served the atmosphere of the play and a sense of group dynamics. His games, or at least the atmosphere that they created, were also visible in the final production.

So how do you get your actors to not only generate material, but generate material that is usable? It is not easy. As Annabel says, "You cannot expect actors to walk into a room and make stuff up" (Arden, 2014). This is true of young people too. You need to provide appropriate exercises to stimulate their imaginations, and facilitate them through the process of creating material. Equally, it is a good idea that these exercises are carefully structured and have boundaries. From my experience the more restrictions an exercise has, the more likely you are to get a thoughtful response. As Annabel says: "If you give too much freedom it is essentially uncomfortable for everybody" (Arden, 2014). Annabel often starts with lots of stuff in the room which has been provided by a designer. Objects and costumes are great starting points for discussion. You might even look at ways that you can manipulate one prop – how can you tell the story in five scenes, each using an umbrella to represent something other than an umbrella, for example. You might end up creating lots and only use some of it, but that is fine. As Annabel says, "It takes time and endless experimenting" (Arden, 2014). Robert clearly uses a great deal of the material that he generates in the rehearsal room, not necessarily as a whole scene, but also to help play existing scenes and create the appropriate atmosphere. A good example would be how to stage two minutes hate. Robert says:

In a traditional process you might sit round and talk about hate, hear some boring anecdotes and then eventually everybody would pretend hatred. And that is alright, but I happen to think it is less interesting when actors are merely pretending. So, instead, we had a hate morning. Everybody had to bring in something that made them feel hatred and share it with the rest of the group. The pressure in the room grew. The actors then walked around the room holding on to that feeling. Then we put some stuff in the middle of the room for them to destroy, like paper, cardboard, and wood. Given the signal, they went absolutely mad. We stood at the back of the room and I remember getting goose bumps because the feeling in the room was so strong. And then we did not really rehearse two minutes hate again after that, we simply had to reconnect with the hate morning and what that had brought up. (Icke, 2014)

His exercises are useful for helping the cast with their performances, as well as creating a shared vocabulary for them based on something they have felt or experienced. The most important thing is to be prepared to experiment. Equally, it is important to remember the bigger picture. Keep your cast in the loop, remind them how this is all fitting together. With young casts, I would suggest something like putting a big list of all the scenes up on the wall so that they can see what is happening at all times. When you are generating material, it is sometimes easy for the young people to lose sight of what they are doing and why, particularly in terms of piecing it all together. The director can often do this quite late in the process, without explaining the choices to the young people, but I would advise against this. Keep them informed throughout, giving a reason for every exercise and involving them in the decision making process. Did it work? Why? If not, why not? As Annabel says: "You have to keep the actors confidence very high. The actors do not necessarily mind being lost if they feel that you don't mind" (Arden, 2104). This is true for young people – but you must tell them and reassure them that being lost is not a problem because it might lead you on an exciting journey of discovery. The young people have the same need as you - they want to make the material with enough time to rehearse it – so remember that you are all in this together.

But how do you deal with your actors when their energy is running low or you are simply not getting anywhere? The key here is variety. Annabel would concur:

Try something different. Sometimes one is tempted to carry on in case something will happen. But from experience, you have

> to turn the problem around, approach it from a different angle
> and hope that something else might work. (Arden, 2014)

If you try to persevere with something that is not working you
will not do yourself or the cast any favours, and it may lead to
other problems like reduced by-in, lack of confidence and even
behavioural issues.

For both Robert and Annabel, successful devising is about casting the right actors. Annabel says:

> Do not cast people who are not fluid and flexible, but, if you
> have to, work very humanly with them and get to the bottom
> of it. What is it? Is it fear? You have to talk to people and reas-
> sure them and make sure there are certain planks in place so
> you can say it is fine. This house stands up, it may have a few
> holes but that is fine. (Arden, 2104)

Robert concurs:

> It is about finding the right people: if you get people who
> are going to resist or want to work in a way that is somehow
> inflexible or ungenerous, they will either be unhappy or get in
> the way of the show's process. (Icke, 2014)

This is not always possible when working with young casts and
so you will need to devote time to encouraging flexibility and
risk taking in the rehearsal room. Many of the exercises on group
dynamics in Chapter 7 will be useful here. Indeed, the cast are
only likely to take risks if they feel safe and supported, so building
trust and confidence, as well as a shared love of the work, is so
important. But it is also important not to be hard on yourself if
things are not going to plan:

> You have to be able to deal with risk and fear and not get
> freaked out or get clammed up. You just have to accept the
> fact that there are days that are just not very good and you
> don't find much. This can go on for several days and the trick
> is to be confident and not to worry. When it works it will
> work fast. (Arden, 2104)

One of the ways of speeding up the process is investing in shared responsibility. It is important for a group not to get isolated from each other in subjective judgment. You have to foster a group sense of professional, not personal, critical judgment. Annabel defines this as a shared language and equates it to playing chamber music:

> A good chamber group, they all know, because they breathe together and they know they rushed that section or they know that section was flat because the syncopation was sufficiently attended too, no matter what. For me, the absolute basis of theatre is rhythm. For the last 20 years I have worked a lot with music and if a group does not have an instinctive shared sense of rhythm, it is much, much harder to make things work. Shared language rests on people's ears being in tune so that they can hear if something is slow or fast, or dull or lively. (Arden, 2014)

This is no different to creating a shared language during rehearsals of a play text. If the group have this shared language, and feel confident to give supportive and constructive feedback, then the process will be so much smoother. For Annabel:

> One thing I find very difficult about traditional theatre is that actors will not comment on other actors' performances. It cannot be discussed because it is too delicate. We've never done that with Complicite because we were making the work together, so we would tussle and comment on each other. You need to say to your actors, "I think it is important that we share our perceptions. What did everybody feel?" We do quite a lot of everybody going round the circle and contributing in an organised way. (Arden, 2014)

It is important early on in the process to ask someone to act as an outside eye. This could be a dramaturg – I would certainly recommend this if you were adapting a long and very complex novel, but this could be anyone who does not have a connection with it.

> As a director, I think you need lots of people you trust to bounce ideas off. You do not always need a dramaturg, but

you do need to be clear about your vision and what that is. I think a designer can have a dramaturgical function because they respond to the material and they have to create a space for that material to live. (Arden, 2014)

For Robert, this was Duncan.

One of the things that initially concerned Annabel when she started devising from text, was about how faithful it needed to be to the original. However, I soon realised that that answer depended on the group that I was working with. I wholeheartedly agree with Annabel:

I do not think it needs to be faithful to the original, as long as you are clear that it is a response to it. I mean that is often to do with how you bill the thing. Is it an adaptation of, or is it based on, or is it inspired by. With *Lion Boy* we had to change a lot. But we were allowed to because we had a very strong relationship with the author and she was involved. She came into rehearsals and we would have long discussions. She loved the final piece – she was absolutely delighted. (Arden, 2014)

Indeed, some of the devised work that I do starts with the text as a stimulus and moves away from the original quite drastically; whereas others have remained fairly faithful to the original, at least in content rather than form.

I have created my own ten-stage process for devising with young people using text as a starting point. This process is as follows:

### 1. Choose your text.

You need to decide what you are starting with – a poem, a recipe, a story, a biography, a play text, a letter, a newspaper article, a novel, a comic. And can this be enhanced with other supporting stimuli – pictures, photographs, music, objects, costumes, films, documents (registers, maps etc.) The list is endless.

### 2. Gather source material.

Once you have decided on your stimulus, you need to introduce it to the young people. That can be as simple as reading a story and showing them any supporting material. It may even involve a visit somewhere. Once you have gathered the material and presented it to them, I would start with a simple brainstorming exercise. Divide the young people up into groups of four or five and give each group five minutes to brainstorm anything and everything that they feel and think about the stimulus. Now use this brainstorm as a starting point for a devised piece. Pass the brainstorm to a different group, so that no one is working on their own brainstorm, and give the pairs a further five minutes to outline two scenes that they want to create, a visual style, and a list of characters to explore from that brainstorm. The essence of this exercise is speed and clarity. Ask each group to feed back their ideas and discuss those that appeal, but explain to the group that no decisions are being made at this point.

### 3. Generate material.

This is where you start creating work and lots of it, so that you can keep the gems and discard the rubbish. This is the point at which I would introduce the phrase about killing babies (see Chapter 7). It is even more applicable to devising than text work, as it is likely that far more will be thrown away than used. The key to generating material is to be as open as possible and to try to engage all of the senses. I would begin by using some of the skeletal scenes from the original brainstorms. A great way to get some of those scenes on their feet is to do a visualisation exercise. The group work individually but simultaneously. Ask them to find a space in the room and explain that you will read them a scene – you will probably want to embellish these as they would have been quite brief. Better still, you could ask for some volunteers to write them up in prose form, asking them to think about making the piece quite descriptive, and from the perspective of a particular character, and use these instead. As you read the prose, ask the group to act it out. What you are interested in seeing is the physical shapes that they create in the space to tell the story. You might then like to repeat the exercise, but split the group in two – one group of performers, the other observers. And then repeat again swapping over so that you can get feedback about was interesting and what people liked. This will then provide moments that could be used as the starting points for further improvisations. Maybe a character stood at a bus stop in the rain. What would happen if you added other characters to that scene? What is she thinking and feeling? Where is the bus? Equally, were there some interesting movement sequences that emerged from the visualisation? What happens when the whole group tap their feet, look at their watch and put up their brolly, rather than the one character. What if they walk in and out at different times, using the same moves, but not playing them in unison? I might do a gesture exercise. In groups, pick one character and find one simple gesture that sums up that character's overall objective in the story. Use the whole body to create the gesture. Think about speed, resistance, being precise and the breath to accompany the movement. Practice it a few times and show it to the rest of the group. Teach the group the gesture. Now add further gestures for smaller objectives. Find a way to link the gestures. Find the largest possible manifestation of those gestures and the smallest possible manifestation of those gestures. Repeat as a score – do the gestures in canon, for example, or do the gestures in increasing size. Just from one simple exercise, the possibilities really are endless. The whole process of generating material is like drawing a picture with a pencil. Some bits look right, others, on closer inspection, need rubbing out and altering slightly or abandoning altogether. But eventually a full and accomplished picture is drawn. You could also use the visualisation exercise to introduce the stimulus text from the outset.

## 4. Character development.

The key to a good devised piece is devoting time to build characters. I usually start with my version of a Noel Greig exercise that he calls 'conjuring up character' (*Playwriting: a Practical Guide*, Noel Greig). Basically it is an exercise that enables the group to think about the detailed traits of their characters. I ask them to write down the answers to a list of questions – some factual, some about the opinions and feelings of their characters, from their gender, age and ethnicity to what they are thinking and feeling at that exact moment in time. By doing this, a whole new set of questions, and essentially possible moments for further exploration, arise. If you start with a story or novel then some of these facets will come from the text, but others will need to be invented based on what you know about the character. I might then begin to improvise actions and scenarios for these characters and find costumes for them in order to unearth more about who they are and where they belong in the world. By answering the questions and doing some improvised character work, your actors will be able to breathe life into their characters.

With these new discoveries, I might then progress to a movement exercise. Ask the group to begin walking around the room as themselves. Notice any tension, the natural tempo or rhythm of their walk, how long their strides are etc. Now ask them to start exploring different ways of moving their feet, toes pointed together or flared out, tiny little steps, big giant steps etc. Give them time to explore how the different options tell a different story and make them feel different. Move up to the legs, trying different things here – stiff legs, bendy legs, springy legs etc. Then on to hips. Are they stiff or loose? Thrust back or forward or to the side? Move up the body, to the chest, the chin, the forehead. What about their eyes? Where do they focus? Up, down or on the horizon? After they have explored their own bodies physically, now ask them to think specifically about their character. Some of the things they have tried so far might feel right. Ask them to go back to them and try them with different combinations of physicality. Remember to think about pace and focus, as that can make all the difference. Again, I would swap in and out so that there is a mix of performers and observers. Since the exercise is completed in silence, I might also ask the observer to pick a performer and narrate his or her actions. They should start with, "I observe..." Encourage them to explain exactly what they see and interpret that. For example, "I see a character who cannot focus on one thing. She seems to be quite absent minded. She is walking slowly which suggests that she has time on her hands. She stops occasionally to look around her and think..." etc. This is particularly useful to heighten the groups' critical faculties, but also for the performers to think about whether their physicality is portraying what they are intending.

As a further character development exercise, I would probably take the students through a version of Jacques Lecoq's seven levels of tension. These have changed and developed during his practice and have been further developed by other practition-ers. The states mentioned below are merely a guideline, to be adapted. Slowly guide the young people through the states so that they become comfortable with them:

- Level 1 – exhausted or catatonic. Ask the students to imagine that they are a jellyfish, as if they have no bones. For this state there should be no tension in the body at all. Tell the group to start in a complete state of relaxation. If they have to move or speak, it is a real effort. How does this affect their speed and their ability to move? What happens when they try to speak?
- Level 2 – laid back. Lots of people live their daily lives operating at this level of tension. Everything they say is cool, relaxed, probably lacking in credibility. They use casual throw-away lines like, "yeah, ok." This state is also sometimes referred to as the Californian – perhaps something to do with the laid back way of life out there?
- Level 3 – neutral. This is exactly what it says. Give nothing away and move with no story behind your movement. There is nothing more, nothing less. The right amount. No past or future. Just totally present and aware. It is the state of tension before something happens. Think of a cat sitting comfortably on a wall, ready to leap up if a bird comes near.
- Level 4 – alert and curious. Look at things. Take notice. Sit down. Stand up. Indecision. Levels 1–4 are human beings' everyday states.
- Level 5 – suspense or the reactive. Is there a bomb in the room? The crisis is about to happen. All the tension is in the body, concentrated between the eyes and in the breath. There is a delay to your reaction. The body reacts.
- Level 6 – passionate. There is a bomb in the room! The tension has exploded out of the body. Anger, fear, hilarity, despair. It is difficult to control. Imagine walking into a room to face a lion, or discovering a snake in the shower.
- Level 7 – tragic. The bomb has gone off! This is the immedi-ate aftermath. The body cannot move, and is in solid tension. Totally and utterly petrified and inconsolable.

After you have taken the participants through the seven levels of tension, try using them in improvisations. Above all, have fun and play around with them. Even if you do not use them in the final piece, they are great for creating a shared vocabulary around character. Throughout the process of generating material and developing character, continue to remind the group that you are on a continual point of departure, not arrival. I have started to film the devising sessions that focus on generating material using an iPad as this provides a helpful reference when consolidating and making choices.

### 5. Consolidate material.

This is now the time to start making some choices. It is time to edit and structure the piece because how we tell the story is as important as the actual story. I would utilise the group for this initially, asking them to tell the story of the piece using one sentence at a time and using a ball. In a circle, one person starts with the ball and says a sentence. They then pass the ball to someone else in the circle who says the next sentence. This is a great exercise to see what the group picks out as being key material or moments, and will help to show you where there are gaps and what needs working on. A shared understanding of the story of the piece is important, and so I would spend considerable time working on this. I might then record the story as a timeline and discuss what is missing; where there is too much exposition (remember that you do not need to explain everything – some things can be shown or hinted at, although subtext is far harder to achieve with devised work); and discuss what material we have already that fits that timeline, and where the gaps are. I would also take time to discuss any material that we really like but does not fit this current timeline. Do we want to find a way to fit it in? Can it be adapted? Or do we need to discard it, despite liking it? I might even encourage the creation of lots of possible narratives at this point, so do the above exercise in three or four smaller groups. And I might get them to storyboard it physically, so using freeze-frames rather than drawing. Having a visual aid of the scenes on the wall would also be useful. I would always test the logic through discussion and by revisiting some of the generated material. I really think that the editing and decision making works best when you do it collectively, but I would make it clear to the group that I will then need to go away and make some decisions without them. If it does not tell the story, do not put it in. Remember, nothing is wasted – any work that does not get on the stage enriches the piece through the character development, texture and bigger picture that it provided.

## 6. What is at stake?

Once you have got a skeletal framework for the piece and have made some concrete decisions about what material will be included and what will not, it is always worth asking yourself this question. Good drama relies on conflict, so where is the opposing force or the tension? And is this resolved? And if so, how? I would also take some time here to think about the opening of the piece. This is really key. It needs to suggest the world of the play, suggest themes and/or mood and atmosphere, include exposition of story and character; and, above all, make an impact – after all, you want your audience to remain hooked. Is there currently any material that does all of this for you? Does it need adapting? Or do you need to take some more time to work on something new?

## 7. Put it all together.

Now is the time to compile a loose script, give the piece a title and consider its order. You have no play text to fall back on when devising, so it is important to ensure a shared understanding of the story of the piece as soon as possible. It is likely that any time line or storyboard that you have created thus far is chronological, so it might be worth playing around with the order of the piece and seeing how that affects the overall story. Although, this will also need some testing in the rehearsal room. Once you have decided on how it is put together, I would definitely now take time to get it into scripted form, even though this will not be the final script. Indeed, *Lion Boy* was never locked down. Annabel said that they changed things on the road all the time. Equally, *1984* was fairly stable by about the third week of rehearsals, but it was never totally locked – it changed in previews in Nottingham and it changed again in rehearsals at the Almeida. As Robert said: "It has never stopped moving because

Duncan and I are both striving to get it perfect, or at least what we think is perfect" (Icke, 2014).

**8. Rehearsals.**

People often forget about this part of the process, or do not allow sufficient time for it, but remember, it has taken this long to get to your final piece. It you are working on an existing play text you have started at this point, so it is wise to start treating the piece as a piece of text now. I would also suggest performing it to an audience as soon as possible, even if it does not feel polished. You, and the young people, are close to the work – usually more so than with a play text, and so you will often lose your ability to be objective. Get some honest feedback. Did they understand it? What did they take from it? What did they enjoy? What could be improved? What did they think and feel? And is this what you wanted them to think and feel?

**9. Restructure and reshape.**

Based on the feedback from your audience, make relevant changes.

**10. Script.**

This is the final version, which equally deserves adequate rehearsal time, so make sure that you factor in enough rehearsal time for really perfecting the piece. You are now ready to start stage one of the five-stage rehearsal process.

This ten-stage process is just one of a million different ways that you can approach devising a piece of work, and it is heavily focused on taking one form of text and adapting that into a play, again one of many different ways of working. For me, the most important thing to remember is that you are going on a long, collaborative journey: at the beginning of that journey your suitcase is empty, but by the time you reach your destination it is full; and you will almost certainly take things out of it and put new things in it along the way.

# 10
## What Now?

One of the things that is crucial, and often eliminated from a youth theatre project, is allowing time after the euphoria has settled to properly analyse the process and the performance. Because everyone has been working so tirelessly to create the performance, and it has always been the end goal, it is easy to just pat ourselves on the back and never actually learn from the experience. This is deadly for two reasons. Firstly, because it teaches the young people that putting on the work is enough, regardless of quality; and secondly, because it presents the industry through rose-tinted glasses. I am not suggesting that the young people should not enjoy the moment, and celebrate the successes, but I am saying that it is easy to get swept up in the adrenalin and excitement and think that the show was a total triumph, whether it was or it was not. Of course it was a success for the young people's friends and family that came to support them, and it was the end of a hard graft for the young people; but it may not have been the best performance ever, and it is useful to consider what everyone has learned from it. From my experience, it is sensible to do any kind of debrief at least a week after the show has finished, to allow the excitement to die down and to give the young people time to properly think about the experience. They will probably all be feeling pretty nostalgic and so an event to bring them back together to properly evaluate the work – what was great about it and what was not so great – might be a good idea. However, it is important to structure this session so that it does not slip into reminiscence and nostalgia, but is instead truthful and beneficial.

I would begin any kind of debrief using the **Rose and Thorn** exercise, giving everyone the opportunity to speak. One at a time, go round the circle and share something that you liked about the process (the rose) and something that you did not like (the thorn). Try to encourage this to be from an individual perspective, and encourage them to fully explain what they mean and/ or give examples. It is a great exercise to get people thinking about the process and is simple enough for everyone to contribute and begin to be reflective. Next, I would use an exercise called **Spectrum of Difference**. Mark the space into three areas – agree, neither agree nor disagree, and disagree. Now give the group a series of statements and ask them to move to the relevant area based on their answer. Some statements might include:

- I was pleased with my overall performance.
- I understood my character and played it to the best of my ability.
- I was confident about what I had to do.
- I worked well as part of the ensemble.
- I enjoyed the process.
- I enjoyed performing.
- There are some things that I would do differently if I could do this again.
- I learnt new things about the craft of theatre.
- I picked up new skills.
- I learnt something about myself.

Once they have decided whether they agree or disagree about a statement, I would begin to question them about why and ask them to give specific examples. Essentially, this is a practical way of generating meaningful analysis and discussion. To finish, I would do a practical exercise that I call **Next Time...** Break the students into smaller groups and have them decide on their top five tips that, with hindsight, they might have given themselves at the beginning of the process, focusing on individual responsibility. Now have the group create five freeze frames to represent those tips. I have often photographed these and shown them to a new group at the beginning of the process, so that it is young people talking to other young people about what can make something a success rather them hearing it from me. Even if I was asking the cast to complete an evaluation form, I would still conduct a practical evaluation first for two reasons. Firstly because coming to an evaluation form cold usually results in sparse answers and box ticking rather than useful examples; and secondly because even if they do complete the actual form sparsely, you will have heard from them verbally about what they felt worked or did not work, so it does not matter, and this can genuinely inform, and improve, your approach next time round.

As well as evaluation, there are other things about putting on a play that need consideration. For example, how do you generate an audience beyond friends and family of the cast? I would argue about why this is important. As long as your cast can generate a good sized audience, who better to have in attendance than those who are simultaneously your biggest supporters and your harshest critics? If you really want to profile the work, then why not invite other youth theatres, local schools or youth groups and/ or other youth theatre practitioners? One of the other issues to contend with is how to deal with young people dropping out. This happens – and sometimes at the very last minute. The first thing to say is do not be disheartened. It is rarely personal, and most often a case of them over committing themselves. The most important thing to remember is to deal with the situation sensitively. Can someone within the current cast take on their role by doubling up? And if is really necessary to bring a new person in, be sure to manage this appropriately so that it does not upset the group dynamic. Finally, it is worth considering whether it is important to invite reviewers and/or agents to see the show. If reviewers, who is likely to come? Not Michael Billington, but maybe a representative from A Younger Theatre, or independent bloggers or the local press. But be sure that you are open to what they have to say, and consider spending some time with your cast discussing the role of the critic and how to deal with criticism.

It seems sensible to leave you with some words of wisdom from the professionals. Below are the tips that they felt were most significant when it comes to directing:

### Indhu Rubasingham.

Indhu has always followed the advice that Mike Leigh gave her on rehearsing a note immediately after giving it: "it is very difficult for actors to remember them, so get into their muscle memory." She also said that it is important, "to trust your gut instinct and keep going. Tenacity is key – just to keep doing it and keep going even when you feel it is really hard and you cannot carry on." (Rubasingham, 2012)

### Richard Eyre.

Richard says: "Just remember that you are not there to answer all the questions, you are there to raise the questions, and it is a bad director, as it is with a bad teacher, who just simply hands out solutions. You have invited a group of people to participate, it is a collaborative venture and it is vital that you recognise that. Any director who does not recognise that, is never going to become a director." (Eyre, 2013)

### Lyndsey Turner.

Lyndsey concurs with Richard: "if you can make friends with the phrase, 'I don't know,' without it compromising who you are, your pride in your job or your ability to move forwards, you are going to have a much better time as a director. You do not need to be a super computer who knows the answer to everything: there are moments in the rehearsal where you can say, 'I have not an idea how to do this.' And those moments might suddenly yield a thousand possibilities." (Turner, 2012)

### Matthew Dunster.

Matthew would leave you with two pointers: one is something that Max Stafford-Clark told him, which is that you cannot cheat the process. By that, like Richard and Lyndsey, he means do not be terrified of not having the answer. He believes that you must find the confidence within yourself to say, "I don't know", and then qualify it by saying, "I don't know yet," and then qualifying it further by saying, "I don't know yet, but we don't need to know yet", or "it will be revealed to us." The other is something that Richard Wilson told him which is that the best way to get anywhere is by agreement: "So find a way to reach unanimous decisions and go on a journey collectively. If anyone is at odds with you, the process will not be harmonious and, by default, neither will the end product." (Dunster, 2012)

**Michael Attenborough.**

Michael also made the assumption when he started directing that the director had to have all of the answers, but he soon realised that this was not the case and urges you to realise this too. For him, it was a huge release to be able to say in rehearsals, "I don't know, let's find out" (Attenborough, 2012) and not be humiliated by that.

**Robert Icke.**

For Robert, although preparation is key, it is important to never forget that theatre is a live art form: "It thrives on the genuinely spontaneous and the virtuosic, which we often overlook in favour of the careful, the logical and the legible." More pragmatically, he would urge you to take pleasure in those moments of difficulty: "feeling properly stuck in a rehearsal can be the best place to be, so enjoy it: it is the moment when the really good ideas come." (Icke, 2014)

**Annabel Arden.**

Annabel says: "I always think of Peter Brook comparing the director to a guide on a journey who does not necessarily know the route. You need to be brave, and trust that the people you have asked to travel with you will provide a lot of the answers. Keep pushing forward, and enjoy every aspect of the journey – especially the difficulties."

It is clear that the role of the director is multilayered and complex; and every director has their own approach to putting on a play. As a director, you are at once a teacher, psychologist, problem solver, relationship manager, project manager, confidante, administrator etc., and this is even truer of a director working with young people. And so my final piece of advice would be to try not to take anything personally and enjoy dabbling in these many and varied roles – what other job would allow you the privilege?

# Glossary of Terms

**Acting Company** – this is the company of actors who will perform your play.

**Action-ing** – this is difficult to define as many practitioners take it to mean different things. In this book action-ing is the technique used by Max Stafford-Clark: breaking up the text into sections, the actor has to find a transitive verb to accompany each individual action.

**Actor** – a person who performs in the play.

**Actor Manager** – a leading actor who sets up their own permanent theatrical company and manages the company's business and financial arrangements, sometimes taking over the management of a theatre, to perform plays of their own choice and in which they will usually star. It was a method of theatrical production and management that started in Elizabethan times but was particularly common in nineteenth-century England.

**Advanced Level** – The General Certificate of Education Advanced Level, commonly referred to as A Level, is an academic qualification offered by educational bodies in the UK to students completing secondary or pre-university education.

**Aeschylus** – the first of the three ancient Greek tragedians whose plays can still be read or performed, the others being Sophocles and Euripides. He is often described as the father of tragedy.

**Almeida Theatre** – A producing theatre in Islington, North London.

**Artistic Director** – An artistic director is the executive of an arts organisation, particularly in a theatre company, that handles the organisation's artistic direction. All of the directors interviewed in this book who have worked or are working as Artistic Directors have done so in building-based producing theatres, that is theatres that produce their own work rather than receiving other people's.

**Assistant Stage Manager** – works in the stage management team, under the direction of the stage manager. Their role varies from job to job and theatre to theatre, but may involve sourcing props for the show or making scene changes during the production.

**Audience** – the people watching the show. This will vary depending on the size of the venue.

**Audition** – an interview for a performing role. The performer will be asked to give a practical demonstration of their suitability and skill.

**Auditorium** – the room in the theatre where the audience sit to see the show.

**Blocking** – the movement and positioning of actors on stage in order to facilitate the performance of the play.

**Box Office** – the place at the theatre where tickets are sold.

**Calling the Show** – this is where the stage manager calls the cues for all transitions in the show, acting as communications hub for the cast and crew.

**Cast** – the actors who perform in the show are collectively referred to as the cast.

**Casting** – a pre-production process for selecting a cast for the show.

**Casting Director** – a person who assists the director with casting.

**Characters** – the fictional people in the play.

**Chorus** – usually a homogeneous, non-individualised group of performers in the play, derived from the Greek concept of the word.

**Classic Text** – noteworthy plays, because of who they are by or because they are an outstanding example of a particular style. They are plays that have lasting worth or with a timeless quality.

**Commissioning** – the act of asking somebody to carry out a service for you. In theatre, this is usually a playwright.

**Complicite** – The British theatre company founded in 1983 by Simon McBurney, Annabel Arden and Marcello Magni.

**Creative Team/Creatives** – the collective group of people in charge of the production, usually comprising the director, designer, movement director, sound and lighting designers etc.

**Critics** – the people who come to the show to review it for newspapers or other media.

**Cues** – a prompt for when to do something. Cues are written in the prompt book so that the stage manager can let the technicians know when sound or lighting changes need to happen.

**Curriculum** – in formal education it is the planned interaction of pupils with instructional content, materials, resources and processes for evaluating the attainment of educational objectives.

**Deputy Stage Manager** – works in the stage management team, under the direction of the stage manager. Their role varies from job to job and theatre to theatre, but usually involves being in the rehearsal room to mark cues in the prompt book and calling the show.

**Designer** – the member of the creative team who is responsible for designing the set and costumes for the show.

**Devising** – the process of creating theatre from an idea, or set of ideas, rather than from a play text.

**Directing** – the art of managing and overseeing the production.

**Director** – the person who is responsible for directing the show.

**Donmar Warehouse** – a producing theatre in Covent Garden, London.

**Dramaturg/Dramaturgy/Dramaturgical** – a professional position within the theatre company that deals mainly with research and development of the play. The responsibilities of a dramaturg vary from one theatre company to the next. They might include the hiring of actors, the development of a season of plays with a sense of coherence among them, assistance with and editing of new plays, helping the director with rehearsals, conducting historical and cultural research into the play and its setting. In the UK, dramaturgs in professional theatres can sometimes also be literary managers.

**Exposition** – the portion of a story that introduces important background information to the audience; for example, information about the setting, events occurring before the main plot, characters' back stories etc.

**Form** – the theatrical style of the piece. Traditionally this is the type of drama that it is – tragedy, comedy, tragicomedy, melodrama, farce, musical etc. – any term that helps define the type of theatre being presented. Some recent drama, however, defies definition – its form is ambiguous or multilayered. Form is complicated because it could be argued that the form of every play is unique because no two plays are exactly alike, but there are certain identifiable characteristics that are common to different plays and it is these characteristics that help to define the form.

**Frantic Assembly** – a theatre company formed by Scott Graham, Steven Hoggett and Vicki Middleton in 1994. Frantic Assembly's unique physical style combines movement, design, music and text.

**Freelance Director** – a director that is self-employed and is hired by a theatre to direct a specific show.

**Greek Theatre/Plays** – a theatrical culture that flourished in ancient Greece in 700 BC. There are a number of classic Greek Plays – comedies and tragedies – that survived from the period and are still performed today.

**Ice Breaker** – a term used to describe the initiation of a social interchange of conversation. To get something started.

**Improvisation** – something that is improvised, in particular a piece of music or drama, is created spontaneously or without preparation.

**Marketing Team** – in simple terms, this is the team who are responsible for spreading the word about the production in order to sell tickets.

**Meet and Greet** – an occasion where all of the cast and creative team come together to meet, usually on the first day of rehearsals.

**MGCfutures Company** – the Education work of the Michael Grandage Company.

**Michael Grandage Company** – a London-based production company set up by Michael Grandage and James Bierman to produce work in theatre, film and television.

**Model Box** – a model of the theatre in which a stage design model is housed. This helps the actors and creative team to see what the stage will look like for the actual production. It is usually produced at a scale of 1:25.

**Monologue** – a long speech by one actor in a play.

**Musical** – a play or film in which singing and dancing play an essential part.

**Narrative** – the storyline.

**Naturalistic** – Naturalism is a movement in European theatre that developed in the late nineteenth and early twentieth centuries. It refers to theatre that attempts to create a perfect illusion of reality on stage. It is commonly used to refer to any theatre that attempts to be realistic in its form.

**New Writing** – This is a very British concept which started at the Royal Court in 1956 with *Look Back in Anger*, by George Osborne. It is plays written by writers, usually young, who see the role of the playwright as being central to theatrical process. New writing is usually plays commissioned by subsidised theatres or companies. In other parts of Europe and the USA the term is virtually unheard of. In these countries, there are merely old plays and new plays.

**Opening Night** – In professional theatre, opening night is the first night after the preview period and is the moment when the play is finally ready. It is also usually the press night as it is traditionally the night when the critics are invited to review the show. It is treated with much celebration and usually involves an invited audience rather than a paying one, and often a celebratory post-show party.

**Performer** – a person who performs in the play (an actor). They may also dance and sing as well as act.

**Physical Theatre** – a genre of theatrical performance that pursues storytelling through primarily physical means.

**Play** – a form of literature written by a playwright, usually consisting of scripted dialogue between characters, intended for theatrical performance rather than just reading.

**Playwright** – the person who writes the play.

**Plot** – the storyline.

**Press Night** – the night when the critics are invited to review the show.

**Preview** – a show during the preview period. This is a select number of the early performances, open to the public but usually at a reduced cost, that precede its official opening. The purpose of previews is to allow the director and the rest of the creative team to identify problems and opportunities for improvement that were not found during rehearsals, and to make any necessary adjustments before the show opens properly.

**Production** – the play.

**Production Manager** – the person who is responsible for realising the director's vision within the constraints of technical and budgetary possibility. This involves coordinating the operations of various production sub-disciplines like lighting, sound, wardrobe, stage management etc.

**Programming** – choosing what plays to put on at the theatre and when.

**Prompt Book** – also called prompt copy, transcript, the bible or sometimes simply "the book," is the copy of a production script that contains the information necessary to create a theatrical production from the ground up. It is a compilation of all blocking, light, speech and sound cues, lists of properties, drawings of the set, contact information for the cast and crew, and any other relevant information that might be necessary to help the production run smoothly.

**Prompt Desk** – also known as Prompt Box or Prompt Corner, it is the place where the prompt, usually the stage manager in the USA or deputy stage manager in the UK, positions themselves in order to coordinate the performance.

**Props** – the objects, or properties other than scenery or costumes, that are used by the actors when performing the play.

**Puppetry** – the art of using puppets (a movable model of a person or animal that is typically moved either by strings controlled from above or by a hand inside it).

**Read-through** – when the cast gather together to read through the play together out loud.

**Rehearsal** – where the actors, under the guidance of the director, practise the play in order to prepare it for an audience.

**Repertoire** – a collection of plays.

**Research** – the investigation into, and study of materials and sources, in order to establish facts and find out new things.

**Revolve** – a circular section of a stage that can be rotated in order to provide a scene change.

**Royal Central School of Speech and Drama** – a drama school in North London.

**Royal Shakespeare Company** – a theatre company dedicated to producing the work of Shakespeare.

**Script** – the play text.

**Season** – a period of the year when selected plays will be programmed and performed. Some theatres will announce the shows that they are putting on as a season of shows rather than individual ones.

**Set** – the physical world of the play suggested by scenery, furniture and other objects.

**Shadow play** – also known as shadow puppetry, is an ancient form of storytelling which uses shadow puppets (flat figures) which are held between a light source and a screen.

**Shakespeare, William** – an English poet, playwright and actor, born in the sixteenth century, widely regarded as the greatest writer in the English language.

**Stafford-Clark, Max** – an English theatre director who co-founded the Joint Stock Theatre Company in 1974, and was Artistic Director of the Royal Court between 1979 and 1993. Known for his technique of Action-ing.

**Stage Manager/Management** – the practice of managing and coordinating the production. The responsibilities and duties of a stage manager vary depending on the stage of the production (i.e., rehearsal or performance) and the scale of the production. A good way to think of it is that the stage manager has overall responsibility to ensure that the director's artistic choices are realised in the final performance, and that these are executed smoothly.

**Stanislavski, Constantin** – a Russian actor and theatre director, famed for his systematic approach to training actors.

**Straight Play** – not a musical.

**Structure** – the building blocks of the play. The play's structure is often dictated by its form.

**Super Objectives** – objectives are the goals that a character wants to achieve in each unit or scene. The Super objective is the goal for the whole play, which will help link the smaller objectives. Part of Stanislavski's system.

**Table Work** – where the directors and actors sit around a table and go through the play line by line to work out its meaning and fully under-stand it. Table work will help the actors to make decisions about how their character is played.

**Tech/Tech Week** – The technical rehearsal, always referred to as "the tech" in professional theatre, is when the technical team and actors come together to work out exactly, in minute detail, how the play is going to work from beginning to end, scene by scene, on the stage with all of the technical elements added to the performance. It usually hap-pens over a tech week.

**Technician/Technical Support** – The person or people who technically operate the show.

**Text** – the play or other form of writing.

**Theatre** – the place in which the play is put on.

**Thespian** – relating to theatre or drama. The term is commonly used to describe a flamboyant actor.

**Through-line** – an acting term that was coined by Konstantin Stanislavski. The idea is that actors should know what their objective is in any scene as well as the line of thought which led from one objective to the next.

**Tricycle Theatre** – a theatre in Kilburn, North London.

**Unit-ing** – when a play is broken down into bite size chunks, or units. Units, also sometimes called beats, were first suggested by Konstantin Stanislavski as a means of helping actors determine the through-line or super objective of their role. A unit is a discrete piece of action in a play-text, marked by a significant change in action.

**Venue** – the place or building that is housing the production. This may or may not be a theatre.

**Wings** – the sides of the stage.

**Workshop/workshopping** – a style of rehearsal that is exploratory in nature, often testing an idea or concept. Workshops can vary in length, but they are usually led by a director or facilitator and there is an emphasis on learning as well as participation. To workshop an idea means to try it out.

**Workshop Audition** – an audition that is less formal than a traditional audition. People would audition in groups rather than individually, often to determine how well they work as part of a team.

**Writer** – somebody who writes. In the theatre, this would be the playwright.

**Young People** – For the purposes of the book, I will define young people as those aged 13 to 18, acknowledging the fact that after a certain age, although legally defined as a child, children prefer the title of young person. All of the exercises in the book would be equally valuable for those who are a little younger and those who are older (most of my work takes place with people aged 14 to 25), although for the much younger, some of them may need adapting slightly.

**Youth Theatre** – a local activity rooted in the community and facilitates the creative interaction of young people through theatre and drama-based activities.

# Further Reading

I have already referenced a number of books that are useful resources for directing, devising and drama games – listed here again alongside others that would be useful for an introduction to directing, devising or working with young people in an arts context. The list is not exhaustive, but merely a suggestion for some useful additional reading:

## Directing

Alfreds, Mike, *Different Every Night*, (London: Nick Hern Books, 2007).

Bogart, Anne, *A Director Prepares*, (London: Routledge, 2001).

Braun, Edward, *The Theatre Director and the Stage*, (London: Methuen Drama, 1982).

Mitchell, Katie, *A Director's Craft*, (London: Routledge, 2009).

Rebellato, Dan and Delgado, Maria (eds), *Contemporary European Theatre Directors*, (Abingdon: Routledge, 2010).

Unwin, Stephen, *So You Want to be a Theatre Director?*, (London: Nick Hern Books, 2004).

## Devising

Graham, Scott and Hoggett, Steven, *The Frantic Assembly Book of Devising Theatre (Second Edition)*, (Abingdon: Routledge, 2014).

Greig, Noël, *Playwriting: A Practical Guide*, (Abingdon: Routledge, 2005).

Heddon, Deirdre and Milling, Jane, *Devising Performance: A Critical History*, (Basingstoke: Palgrave Macmillan, 2005).

Oddey, Alison, *Devising Theatre: A Practical and Theoretical Handbook*, (Abingdon: Routledge, 1996).

## Games

Farmer, David, *101 Drama Games and Activities*, (Lulu.com, 2011).

Farmer, David, *101 More Drama Games and Activities*, (CreateSpace Independent Publishing Platform, 2012).

Johnston, Chris, *Drama Games for Those that Like to Say No*, (London: Nick Hern Books, 2010).

Swale, Jessica, *Drama Games for Classrooms and Workshops*, (London: Nick Hern Books, 2009).

Swale, Jessica, *Drama Games for Devising*, (London: Nick Hern Books, 2012).

## Practitioners

Theatre practitioners are directors, writers and actors, or all three, who simultaneously create work and produce a theoretical discourse to inform that work. Reading about other practitioners is useful in informing your own style/practice.

### *Antonin Artaud*

Artaud, Antonin, *The Theatre and its Double,* (London: Alma Classics, 2013).

### *Augusto Boal*

Babbage, Frances, *Augusto Boal*, (Abingdon: Routledge, 2004).
Boal, Augusto, *The Rainbow of Desire: The Boal Method of Theatre and Therapy*, (Abingdon: Routledge, 1994).
Boal, Augusto, *Games for Actors and Non-Actors*, (Abingdon: Routledge, 2002).
Boal, Augusto, *Theatre of the Oppressed*, (London: Pluto Press, 2008).

### *Bertolt Brecht*

Brecht, Bertolt, *Brecht on Theatre*, (London: Bloomsbury Methuen Drama, 2014).

### *Constantin Stanislavski*

Benedetti, Jean, *Stanislavski: An Introduction*, (London: Methuen Drama, 2008).
Stanislavski, Constantin, *An Actor's Handbook: An Alphabetical Arrangement of Concise Statements on Aspects of Acting*, (London: Methuen Drama, 1990).
Stanislavski, Constantin, *An Actor's Work: A Student's Diary*, (Abingdon: Routledge, 2009).
Stanislavski, Constantin, *Creating a Role*, (London: Bloomsbury Academic, 2013).
Stanislavski, Constantin, *An Actor Prepares*, (London: Bloomsbury Academic, 2013).

### *Jerzy Grotowski*

Grotowski, Jerzy, *Towards a Poor Theatre*, (London: Methuen Drama, 1975).

## *Vsevolod Meyerhold*

Braun, Edward, *Meyerhold: A Revolution in Theatre*, (London: Methuen, 2006).

Meyerhold, Vsevolod, *Meyerhold on Theatre*, (London: Methuen, 1969).

Meyerhold, Vsevolod, *Meyerhold Speaks/Meyerhold Rehearses*, (Abingdon: Routledge, 1997).

Pitches, Jonathan, *Vsevolod Meyerhold*, (Abingdon: Routledge, 2003).

# Index